Wanted

Friends and Footwashers

Revised & Expanded Edition

Cardinal
Seán Patrick O'Malley, OFM Cap.

With a Foreword by
Cardinal José Tolentino Mendonça

Paulist Press
New York / Mahwah, NJ

Cover art: "Jesus Washing Peter's Feet," by Ford Madox Brown 1852, © Tate Gallery, London. Used with permission.
Cover design by Sharyn Banks
Book design by Lynn Else

Originally published as *Procura-se Amigos e Lavadores de Pés* copyright © 2019, Instituto Missionário Filhas de São Paulo-Paulinas Editora, Rua Francisco Salgado Zenha, 11–2685-332 Prior Velho–Portugal

Library of Congress Control Number: 2022930525

ISBN 978-0-8091-5636-8 (paperback)
ISBN 978-0-8091-8798-0 (e-book)

Published by Paulist Press
997 Macarthur Boulevard
Mahwah, New Jersey 07430
www.paulistpress.com

Printed and bound in the
United States of America

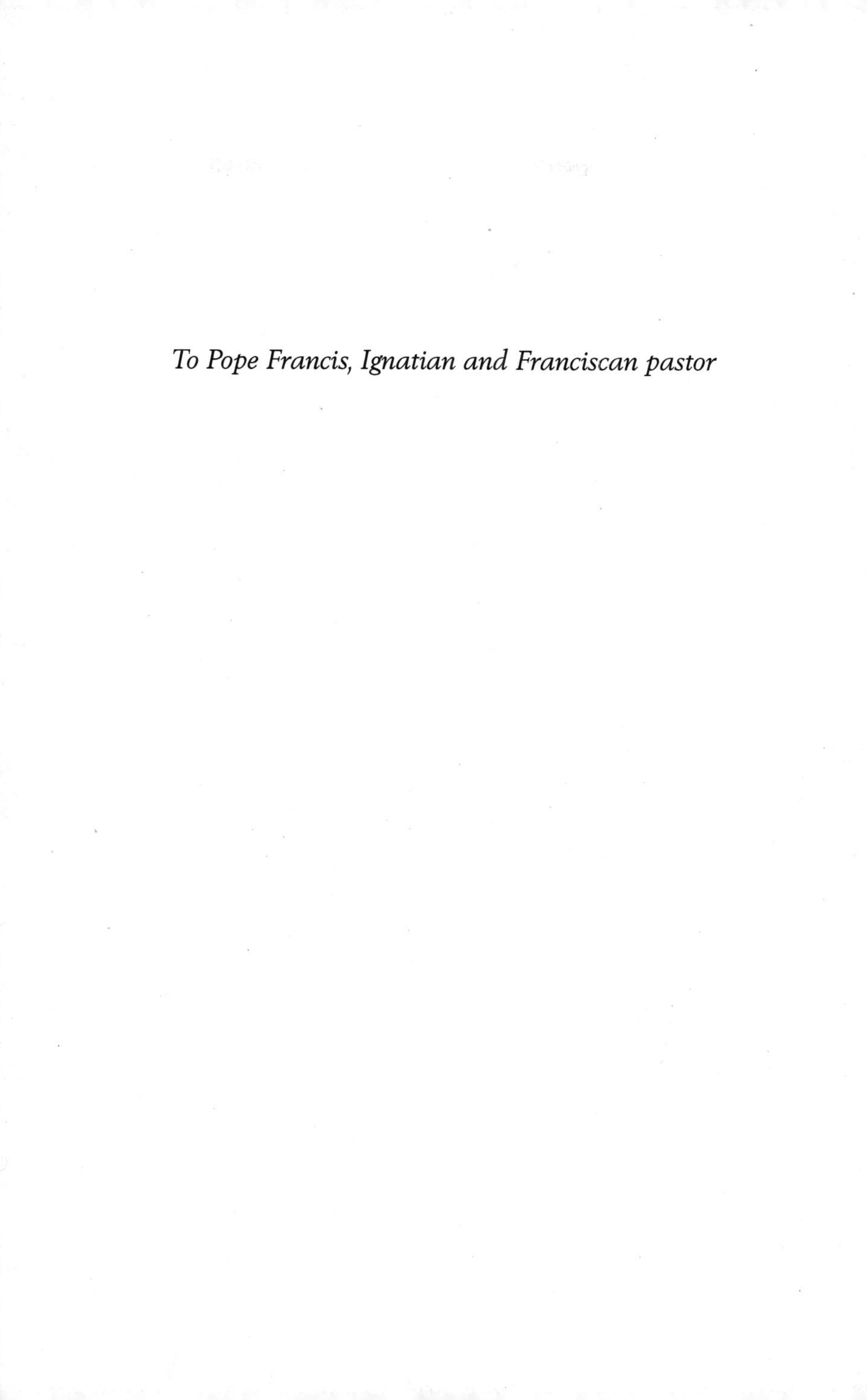

To Pope Francis, Ignatian and Franciscan pastor

CONTENTS

Part II: To the Rhythm of Liturgy and Mission

FOREWORD

Humor too converts.

If a survey on spiritual life included a question about what state of being is mostly associated with repentance and conversion, I am convinced the overwhelming response would be grief for evil done, remorse, and tears. Tradition is full of relevant examples along these lines, and we all know, not least from personal experience, how acutely effective this kind of grief can be in the process of inner transformation. Scripture broadly confirms this, as can be seen in the Book of the Prophet Joel, which we read at the beginning of Lent:

> Yet even now, says the LORD,
> return to me with all your heart,
> with fasting, with weeping, and with mourning....
>
> Between the vestibule and the altar
> let the priests, the ministers of the LORD, weep.
> (Joel 2:12, 17)

Or as it resounds in the beatitude uttered by Jesus, "Blessed are you who weep now" (Luke 6:21). Therefore, the importance of crying was naturally transmitted to Christian spirituality. Tears have become the expression of this "sorrow according to God," which is not, as Origen was the first to explain, any voluntary sorrow but "a permanent grief brought about by the grief of sin." For centuries, liturgy has maintained prayers implicitly imploring the gift of tears: "Oh God, grant that we cry abundantly over the evils that we have done, so that we may merit the grace of your consolation." Feelings of guilt were (and are) also seen as a precious trial for the soul, an itinerary that reconciles us with God's desire.

The philosopher Emil Cioran once wrote that the greatest gift of religion can only be that it teaches us to weep. He explained, "Tears are that which can make us holy after we have been human." Which is true, but not completely. Precisely what failed in a certain representation of Christian spirituality was to submit "sorrow according to God" not as a means but as a purpose, just about losing sight of the experience of grace, mercy, and redemption.

However, when we come across the inspiring words of Cardinal Seán O'Malley—of which this wonderful book that the reader is holding is a great example—there is a particular element that draws one's attention. Its goal is also to assist our conversion, but rather than tears, the chosen instrument is humor. This shows the depth, the originality, and the refinement of his wisdom. This is not a simple and harmless humor casually repeated as a cliché. One need not look further than the first story he tells about his experience with Bishop Gerardi to understand how his wit comes into play. While once living in a rural area, the bishop

> would celebrate Mass each morning in the cathedral. Each day upon leaving the cathedral to cross the plaza, he would see a man named Santiago laying on a bench, dirty, unshaven, covered with

> old newspapers. The poor man smelled of alcohol and his eyes were bloodshot. Despite his condition, he would always politely stand and with great affection greet the bishop. Yet one day, crossing the plaza, the bishop was dismayed not to see Santiago. Weeks passed with still no sign of him, until one day the bishop met Santiago walking down the street, but at first he did not recognize him. Santiago was freshly shaven, his hair cut. He wore a clean suit and new shoes and had a Bible tucked under his arm. After realizing who he was, the bishop exclaimed, "What happened?" "I was saved!" Santiago answered. The bishop profusely congratulated him and said farewell.
>
> A month later, the bishop left the cathedral only to find Santiago once again in deplorable condition back on his old bench. "Santiago, what happened?" "*Monseñor,*" he replied, "I have returned to the one true Church."

This is a type of humor that amuses, yes, but it can also make us think. It can cut through our entrenched certainties, question our sleepwalking existence, rattle our good conscience, and take away the clichés with which we so often reduce the religious experience. The humor used by Cardinal O'Malley is not meant to be delicious. It may be just that, but the goal is quite different. It is meant to crack us open, expose us for who we are, lead us to renounce the Gnostic or Manichean temptation that separates the supernatural action from our reality as it is, with its roughness and infamy. Worst of all would be to live only in a regime of appearances, without allowing God's grace to touch our truth.

In Cardinal O'Malley's writings and in his preaching, there are three qualities that are characteristically all his own.

One of them is this incisive sense of humor. It is a tool for wisdom through which we can see both the essence of simplicity and good nature that are typical of a Capuchin friar. It is also, as novelist Flannery O'Connor has shown, useful in dismantling the self-justifying discourse often espoused by believers. O'Connor wrote that "the more the writer wishes to make the supernatural apparent, the more real he has to be able to make the natural world, for if the readers don't accept the natural world, they'll certainly not accept anything else." In the case of the Cardinal, I would still add the old tradition of *risus paschalis*, "the Easter laugh." In the past, the priest would sometimes seek to amuse the faithful during the Easter homily, making them laugh with anecdotes or stories so that the paschal joy might be shared by all. Indeed, there is a paschal spirit that runs through O'Malley's work. His insistence that paschal dynamics provoke a radical inversion in our way of celebrating the faith is nicely expressed in this very short dialogue with a mystic. A man asked, "I have committed many sins. If I repent, will God forgive me?" The mystic replied, "No. You will repent if he forgives you."

Another important feature in the elaboration of his speech is the first person singular, because the word of the present Archbishop of Boston never advances by abstractions, but instead is rooted in the witness of Christianity. He exposes himself, speaks about himself and his spiritual biography, recounts encounters, reinterprets history, reads the signs of Christ in time, as is described in the First Letter of John: "We declare to you what was from the beginning, what we have heard, what we have seen with our eyes, what we have looked at and touched with our hands, concerning the word of life" (1 John 1:1). It is thus an existentially committed discourse and one that beckons the same from the reader. For O'Malley, words are not a garment behind which to hide. They are a straightforward exercise, a dialogical practice, life's breath. Reading his words, we have the feeling of sitting next to him, in conversation. The result of this is that the subject matter, whatever it may be, becomes relevant for all. In this book, for example, his thoughts on the ministry of bishops and their vocation and mission in the Church may seem appropriate for a narrow, specific readership. Yet he presents these reflections in a way so that his wisdom becomes relevant for all.

His willingness to share his personal experience allows us to come to know the unique personality of Cardinal O'Malley, to be fascinated by the breadth of his pastoral understanding and the beauty of the human relations heritage he has been weaving. We realize the immense world of culture and erudition that he unpretentiously carries with him while also getting a feeling for the freedom of his heart and the pulsating evangelical wisdom that resonates through him.

But perhaps the main reason—and this is the third identifying characteristic—is his love for the word of God. As he reminds us, God speaks to us through his word. We are called to live our lives probing the Scriptures in search of God's voice and face. As such, the daily study of the word of God is the first task, the *primum officium* that we have to assume. It is from the word that everything dawns. It is the unceasing source of knowledge of Christ. That is why Cardinal O'Malley puts forward that we must fall on our knees to feel the Word of God and our theology must be a "theology on ones knees." I believe this is the secret that makes him one of the great masters of our time.

Whoever reads this book shall not forget it!

Cardinal José Tolentino Mendonça

PREFACE

Shortly after being named archbishop of Boston, I received a letter from a woman in Ireland, whom we might describe as unclaimed treasure. She wrote to me because she thought the new archbishop would be the right person to find her a husband in America. She wanted a hard-working man, not given to drink and who faithfully adhered to the precepts of the Church. Today there are many online services that help people identify a spouse. This has enabled people to get quite particular. Usually they're looking for a "nonsmoking vegan who enjoys movies and travel."

Many online resources exist just to match workers with employers. In these "want ads," a potential employer may be looking for a babysitter with references, or someone adept at carpentry or landscaping. Our law enforcement agencies have their own kind of "want ads" that we call "wanted posters." These notices, complete with unflattering photographs of the criminals, can be seen online in the FBI's top ten most wanted or on the walls of the post office. In the Wild West of history and fiction, these wanted posters often declared in bold print, "Wanted, dead or alive. Reward for information leading to the capture of this individual. Failure to report will result in imprisonment." Even Harry Potter is on a wanted poster in the Deathly Hallows—"undesirable number one."

I like to imagine that if Jesus were to use a classified ad to call people to discipleship ministry, it might read like the title of this book, *Wanted: Friends and Footwashers*. These are the necessary attributes that Jesus asks of his apostles in his last testament, his farewell at the Last Supper.

The Lord tells the apostles that they are to be his friends, not functionaries. That is the difference between being a shepherd and a hireling. The new commandment, "love one another as I have loved you" (John 15:12), is telling us that our deepest identity is found in friendship with Christ and with each other.

The Lord is not calling us to be fair-weather friends but the kind of friends willing to lay down our lives. Our interior life is meant to cultivate this friendship that will allow us to produce the fruits of joy that Jesus speaks about in his final instructions to us.

At the wedding feast of Cana there were six stone water jars. At the Last Supper (also a kind of wedding feast), there was probably just one. Jesus did not change water into wine at the Last Supper; he was too busy changing wine into blood. Instead, he used the water in that stone jar to wash the feet of his disciples and then invited them to do the same, to become footwashers. He wanted his apostles, his friends, to stop fighting over the first places at the table and start fighting over the towel.

The meditations in this little book are based on the job description that Jesus gave us at the Last Supper, that of friend and footwasher. Sharing these thoughts with my listeners and readers has certainly made me more aware of my own inadequacies in living up to these challenging ideals in my life and ministry.

Some years back the Portuguese Bishops' Conference blithely invited me to preach a retreat to them at Fatima. After my last conference, I announced that I was immediately returning home to Fall River, Massachusetts, in observance of the stern admonition of our old Capuchin constitutions that declare that after a friar preaches a retreat, he should depart immediately and return to the monastery so as not to undo with his bad example any good he may have accomplished by his preaching. It seems to have worked. They invited me back.

It is indeed a great privilege to be asked. I accepted this invitation in faith and humility, knowing that the real retreat master is always the Holy Spirit, whose gentle breeze moves our hearts to greater love and fidelity. The retreat also afforded me the opportunity to spend time in Fatima and to reconnect with my brother bishops in Portugal. God in his loving Providence has connected my life and ministry with Portugal and the Lusophone world. To me it has been such a source of joy and blessing.

My time in Portugal also resulted in this book. I express my gratitude to Maria Cortez de Lobão and the Daughters of St. Paul for their invaluable help in preparing this volume. I also thank my dear friend, Cardinal José Tolentino Mendonça, for his kind and thoughtful foreword.

In Fatima, I joined my prayers and supplications to the countless pilgrims who find healing and renewal in that holy place. I pray for our beloved Church and all those called to roles of leadership in our community of faith. May Our Lady of Fatima, the handmaid of the Lord, help all of us to grow in our capacity to be friends and footwashers.

PART I

Friends and Footwashers

1

MERCY

In recent years, the Church in Central America has produced many martyrs. The most famous of these is the archbishop of San Salvador, Monseñor Oscar Romero, who was canonized along with Pope Paul VI in October 2018. Another bishop martyred for his defense of human rights was Bishop Juan Jose Gerardi Conedera of Guatemala who worked for years among indigenous people. In the 1970s, Bishop Gerardi gained government recognition of the indigenous languages as official languages. In 1988, he was appointed to the government's National Reconciliation Commission to begin a process of accounting for abuses during the civil war.

In 1998, Bishop Gerardi presented the Church's sponsored report on the victims of the civil war, "*Guatemala: Nunca Más*" ("Guatemala: Never Again"). Two days after presenting the document, he was brutally murdered in his garage, beaten to death. He was so disfigured that they could identify him only because of his episcopal ring. Eventually, three army officers were convicted of the crime.

I met Bishop Gerardi because I lived with him when I was the apostolic visitator for the Guatemalan seminaries. He was a delightful man, full of stories and anecdotes from years of pastoral ministry. He told me how when he was bishop in a rural area, he would celebrate the Mass each morning in the cathedral. Each day upon leaving the cathedral to cross the plaza, he would see a man named Santiago laying on a bench, dirty, unshaven, covered with old newspapers. The poor man smelled of alcohol and his eyes were bloodshot. Despite his condition, he would always politely stand and with great affection greet the bishop. Yet one day, crossing the plaza, the bishop was dismayed not to see Santiago. Weeks passed with still no sign of him, until one day the bishop met Santiago walking down the street, but at first did not recognize him. Santiago was freshly shaven, his hair cut. He wore a clean suit and new shoes and had a Bible tucked under his arm. After realizing who he was, the bishop exclaimed, "What happened?" "I was saved!" Santiago answered. The bishop profusely congratulated him and said farewell.

A month later, the bishop left the cathedral only to find Santiago once again in deplorable condition back on his old bench. "Santiago, what happened?" "*Monseñor*," he replied, "I have returned to the one true Church."

Santiago, of course, is right. The true Church is made up of sinners. The Good Shepherd prioritizes the lost sheep as the most important pastoral goal. Jesus came as the physician for the sick. He came to reveal the merciful face of the Father. Pope Francis's Year of Mercy was, in my experience, the most successful holy year the Church has had in my lifetime. People resonated with the theme. Nothing is more central to the gospel than mercy and forgiveness.

The parable of the prodigal son helps us to glimpse the mercy of God. It's the story of the anatomy of sin and evil disguised as something good—the liberty of an individual's rights to an inheritance—the disguised ingratitude of a young man who wants to make his life without the father, without God.

In this parable there is a moment of discovery—the money runs out, life is no longer fun. We see how sin does not bring happiness, only emptiness. But grace touches the heart of the sinner so that he desires to return to his father's house. The prodigal son begins rehearsing his lines, like the young man waiting in line nervously to go to confession: Father, I have sinned against heaven and against you.

Indeed, the most beautiful part of this parable is where our Lord describes the old man, the father searching the horizon. When he sees his son, he runs out to meet him. The boy is dragging his feet, walking slowly. The mercy of God always runs swiftly even when our repentance moves slowly with leaden feet.

Oftentimes we forget the context of this beautiful parable. Jesus tells this parable in response to the Pharisees who criticize Jesus for eating with sinners. The parable could have been titled "the story of the elder brother," who in a certain way represents those Pharisees.

We must ask ourselves the question, what did the older brother do to try to prevent the prodigal son from leaving home on his ill-founded plans? The older brother is very quick to judge and condemn his brother and tries to dissociate himself from him. He says, "That son of yours." The attitude of the father is to go out and seek, to bring his sons home whether it be the prodigal son returning after squandering all of his inheritance or the older hard-working son returning from the fields, indignant when he realizes that his father is celebrating his brother's return. The father shows mercy to the prodigal son and tries to teach mercy to his other son. He tells the elder, "You are always with me, everything I have is yours. But your brother was dead and has come back to life. Rejoice!"

Brian Moore, the twentieth-century Irish writer, wrote a novel that contains an amusing scene describing an encounter between a parish priest and one of his worldly parishioners.

Her name is Mrs. Brady and she is the owner of what the Irish politely refer to as "a bad house." It seems that Mrs. Brady is getting on in years and is beginning to think about returning to the Church to receive the sacraments and to try to clean up her obituary. She decides that she will present a church with a new communion rail: "wrought iron from Spain, all the finest work." So, she goes to the priest and offers to pay all the expenses. The pastor immediately recognizes her and, filled with holy indignation, sternly asks her, "Do you think I'll have the good people of this parish kneeling down on their bended knees to receive the Body and Blood of Jesus Christ with their elbows on the wages of sin and corruption?"

Mrs. Brady simply looks calmly into his eyes and responds, "Father, where do you think the money came from that Mary Magdalene used to anoint the feet of Our Blessed Lord? It didn't come from selling apples."

The moral of the story is indeed that Jesus was the friend of sinners. He received those who no one else would receive. He was a friend of publicans and prostitutes, of Zacchaeus, of Levi, and of many other persons whom respectable people rejected. Jesus called them to conversion, to friendship, and even to ministry. Often, he celebrated their change of heart with feasts or banquets. The Gospels are full of these conversion stories.

Jesus says there's more joy over one sinner who repents than over ninety-nine of the just. The Good Shepherd leaves the ninety-nine sheep to go in search of the one lost sheep. Today we would probably say the lost sheep should be a tax write-off or an insurance claim. But for Jesus, the lost sheep was the priority. Pope Francis is often challenging us to go in search of those on the periphery, those who are forgotten, rejected, far away.

It's bad enough that Jesus has this attitude, but what's really alarming is that he expects us to be of like mind. In the parable of the unjust steward, Jesus tells the story of a man who owes a fortune to his king. In today's money he would have owed the king many millions of dollars. Even if he won the lottery, he wouldn't have enough money to pay off such an enormous debt. The man asked for clemency and the king forgave him everything. But as soon as he left the king's presence, he ran into a colleague who owed him a denarius, one day's wages. Although the man asked for mercy, he threatened him, then had him thrown into debtors' prison.

How many times are we like that unjust servant? God has forgiven us so much and how many times are we unwilling to forgive each other the petty offenses we inflict on one another. Jesus is letting us know that the minimal requirement to be his disciple is that we be merciful and ready to forgive each other. Be perfect as your Heavenly Father is perfect. He makes his sun to shine on the good and evil. He sends his rain equally on the just and the unjust.

When Jesus teaches his disciples how to pray, he includes a very dangerous petition in the Our Father: "Forgive us our trespasses as we forgive those who trespass against us." Jesus is not only telling us that we must pardon buddies; he is telling us how: in the same way that God pardons.

A certain existentialist author from France, Jean Anouilh, included the idea of this dangerous petition from the Our Father in one of his plays. As Louis Évely describes the scene in *That Man Is You*, "The good are densely clustered at the gate of heaven, eager to march in, sure of their reserved seats, heated up and bursting with impatience. All at once, a rumor starts spreading; It seems he's going to forgive those others, too! For a moment, everyone's dumbfounded...'After all the trouble I went through?!'...Exasperated, they work themselves into a fury and start cursing God, and at that very instant they are damned. That was the final judgment." "Blessed are the merciful, for they will receive mercy" (Matt 5:7).

At one point in the Gospels, the Pharisees say that only God can forgive sins. They mean it as a criticism of Jesus's claim to forgive sins, but actually it's a very good description of God. Only God really knows how to forgive. It is said if we are Irish, we don't get mad, we just get even. An Irish Alzheimer's is when a person forgets everything but the grudges. They also say that women forgive but don't forget. Whereas men are often so self-centered that we forget without taking the time and the trouble to forgive.

Human forgiveness is often a very unpleasant experience, a bitter memory. The superiority and condescension of the one who is pardoning often crushes the one who's receiving that pardon. There may be forgiveness but not consolation or encouragement. Whereas when God forgives, he forgives us as the Holy Father says, with a caress. He does not humiliate us, he humbles himself. The father of the prodigal son doesn't want to hear one word about the whole episode; he simply wants to have a banquet. Only God can transform pardon into something glorious to remember.

God is so happy to absolve us, those who give him the joy of forgiving; he treats us not as difficult and disagreeable children, but as children who are pampered, encouraged, understood. We could proclaim, O *Felix Culpa* (Oh Happy Fault). If we weren't sinners and didn't need forgiveness more than we need bread, we would never have any way of imagining how much and how deep God's love is for us.

In the conversions of Saul and Levi, who become St. Paul and St. Matthew, Jesus surprises them in the very act of sinning. He forgives them, calls them to conversion, and makes them disciples. He calls them from sin to fidelity to ministry. Matthew leaves the pile of money in the tax collector's booth where he's been exploiting the poor and goes and celebrates a banquet to mark his conversion. Imagine someone asking, "What's all the partying about over at so-and-so's house?" And being told in reply, "Oh, he just went to confession and he's celebrating."

In the episode of the Gospel of John about the woman caught in adultery, we see how they tried to discredit Jesus by bringing him an adulteress and asking if she should be stoned. Our Blessed Savior reads their treacherous hearts and says, "Let anyone among you who is without sin be the first to throw a stone at her" (8:7). Afterward, Jesus begins to write on the ground with his finger. It's the only time in the Gospels that Jesus writes anything. We don't know for certain what he was writing, but the Fathers of the Church tell us he was writing the sins of those men who brought the adulterous woman there. In silence they begin to sneak away, starting with the eldest. When they see their own sins, the stones begin to fall from their hands. They had forgotten that they too needed God's mercy.

God in his mercy has given us a sacrament to concretize his forgiveness. In confession, we write our sins on the sand, we contemplate our guilt and the stones fall from our hands, and then Jesus erases our sins. The sacrament of confession is where we experience God's loving forgiveness and where Jesus teaches us to be loving and compassionate to others. Pope Francis talks about his own personal vocation as taking place in the context of the sacrament of confession. As a young man, he was going off to a picnic with a lot of his friends when suddenly he felt an urge to go to church and receive the sacrament of confession. From that moment on, he felt that God was calling him to a special vocation. It was on the Feast of St. Matthew, the tax collector whom Jesus invited to be a disciple. Many years later, when Padre Jorge Bergoglio was named bishop, he chose as his motto *miserando atque eligendo*, which comes from the office for the Feast of St. Matthew and means "seeing him through the eyes of mercy he chose him," harkening back to the moment when

Jesus saw Matthew the tax collector and called him to be an apostle.

The sacrament of God's mercy affords us the opportunity to review our life in the light of the gospel and respond to the call of an ongoing conversion, overcoming sin and selfishness in our lives so that we will be able to love in an unselfish way, and generously and joyfully embrace the mission that God has entrusted to us.

In the Gospels, Jesus says that we must not be like the Pharisees were, only concerned about appearances. We must strive to clean the inside of the cup, to transform our hearts by God's grace. In the sacrament of confession, with gratitude and contrition, we draw near the throne of God's mercy, where the merciful Christ, the friend of sinners, makes himself present to us to show us his mercy and to teach us how to be merciful with others.

Many years ago, in prerevolutionary Cuba, there was a popular radio program called "La Muralla," which caused quite a stir in the Catholic community. It was the story of a wealthy Catholic family: husband, wife, and six children. Every Sunday, the whole family went to Mass. Everyone received communion except the father. This was a great source of embarrassment and anxiety to his wife and children. They often tried to convince their dad to go to confession so that he could receive communion with them. He refused always. The years passed and when he was dying, his wife and children sent for the parish priest who came to administer the last sacraments. After the man received the sacraments, he called his family around his deathbed. He explained to them how much he'd wanted to receive communion with them, but he could not because he had falsified a will. He explained that all the money, the beautiful house, and the good life were the result of this crime. Actually, all these things should belong to a distant cousin of theirs. He said he knew that if he confessed the sin, he would have to make restitution and return what was stolen and he wasn't ready to do that. Shortly thereafter the man died. But from that time on it was his wife and children who stopped going to communion because they weren't ready to return their fortune either.

It's so easy to judge others severely, but it's only when we find ourselves in the same circumstances that we discover our own weakness.

The ancient Greeks had a temple known as the Delphic Oracle. The sage inscription on the front of the temple said γνωθι σε αυτόν, *gnōthi seauton*, "know thyself." Personal conversion always begins with self-knowledge. In *The Interior Castle*, St. Teresa of Avila describes her own spiritual journey and speaks of meeting giant monsters along the way. The inner journey is often very difficult, but as part of our vocation as Christians, we must recognize our own weaknesses and faults.

Nevertheless, the Catholic attitude toward sin is not one of obsession. In Nathaniel Hawthorne's novel *The Scarlet Letter*, a woman who commits adultery is compelled to wear an enormous red letter *A* sewn onto her dress, marking her as an adulteress.

François Mauriac, a famous French Catholic writer, contrasts this Calvinistic attitude with the Catholic notion of sin. In one of his novels, he describes a fugitive from the police who runs into a Calvinist Church and says, "Help me. I have just killed a man in a fight." The sacristan exclaims in horrid alarm, "Get out of here, you murderer. I'm going to call the police." The man runs out, crosses the street, and goes into a Catholic Church. In the darkened church he sees a red light in the confessional. He goes in and says to the priest, "Father help me, I just killed a man." The priest responds, "How many times?"

The Church has a lively consciousness of sin but is not obsessed by sin. We profess, "Where sin doth abound, there doth grace more abound." The grace of God is sufficient. His mercy can cure us; it is stronger than sin.

I've always liked the story about the Irish farmer who lived on the banks of a river. Every week his pastor would arrive at the riverbank and shout, "Of the same" and a voice echoed back from the other side, "The same." The old farmer was so curious that he got up enough courage to ask the priest what it was all about. His pastor told him that since he was the only priest in that village, this was the way that he made his weekly confession. He would go down to the one riverbank—the priest in the neighboring village would be on the other side—and he would shout "Of the same," meaning the same sins. Father O'Brien would shout back "The same" meaning the same penance.

However, we must never allow our confessions to become routine, even if they at times are frequent. Every confession, as with every communion, is a loving encounter with the merciful Lord who binds up our wounds, puts us on his mount, and takes us to a safe place, just as the Good Samaritan did with the man left half dead on the road to Jericho. The risen Lord appeared to his disciples on Easter, breathed upon them, and said, "Receive the Holy Spirit. If you forgive the sins of any, they are forgiven them" (John 20:22–23).

We must learn to love the sacrament of God's mercy where the Lord is always calling us to deepen our conversion, to grow in our capacity to love and serve, and to be more generous in fulfilling our mission in the world. In a world where there are so many divisions, hatred, racism, and envy, we need the peace and reconciliation that Christ brings to the world. In the sacrament of his mercy, we learn to be instruments of that peace in a world that is so tragically divided and so hungry for mercy and love.

"Give thanks to the Lord, for he is good; for his steadfast love endures forever" (Ps 106:1).

2

NAZARETH AND CAPERNAUM

St. Jerome used to call the Holy Land the Fifth Gospel and I believe he is right. Visiting the various places mentioned in the Gospels makes it all come alive. Even without visiting firsthand, these locations can take on special meaning. We have named the chapel at the pastoral center in Boston the Bethany Chapel because at Bethany, Jesus went to be at home with his dear friends Lazarus, Mary, and Martha. Martha's words from St. John's Gospel grace the wall of the chapel in nearby Braintree: *Magister adest et vocat te,* "The Master is here and is calling you."

When I was studying at St. Fidelis of Sigmaringen Seminary, affectionately called the Capuchin Agricultural School, I was part of the group that the rector dubbed "the Gerasenes." Father Rector would often rouse us at 2:00 in the morning because our herd of swine would escape from their corral and head to the parish cemetery. Like those swine filled with a legion of demons hurling themselves into the sea, our pigs descended upon the fresh graves of pious German farmers. There in the middle of the night, dressed in our night shirts and wielding baseball bats and 2 x 4s we would drive the beasts back to their muddy pens.

Still, in all, the Holy Land is the Fifth Gospel. Today, I would like to reflect on the theological meaning insinuated by two different venues in the Gospel.

According to the Gospels, Jesus's earthly life begins in Bethlehem and ends in Jerusalem, but the truth is that Jesus spent very little time in those two cities. Most of Jesus's life was spent in Nazareth and Capernaum. Indeed, Jesus was known as the Nazarene. The Gospel of Luke tells us Jesus gave his first sermon in the synagogue in Nazareth. At the end, he powerfully tells those gathered listening to him, "Today this scripture has been fulfilled in your hearing" (4:21).

The Gospel continues in another vein if we read on. First, Luke comments that "all spoke well of him and were amazed at the gracious words that came from his mouth." But it did not take long before they were saying, "Is not this Joseph's son?" "Do here also in your hometown the things that we have heard you did at Capernaum." Jesus replies by pointing out that prophets are not accepted in their hometowns and uses Elijah and Elisha, who worked miracles for foreigners, as illustrations.

The Spanish have a great proverb to describe someone who changes from one place to another in the hopes of changing themselves. They say, "*La fiebre no está en las sábanas.*" "The fever is not in the bed sheets." Sometimes the venue is part of who we are: "You can take the boy out of Southie, but you can't take Southie out of the boy." In Jesus's life, these two places—Nazareth and Capernaum—are so important to his identity and ministry. After Jerusalem, they are the cities most mentioned in the Gospels. The concordance shows that Nazareth appears fifteen times and Capernaum is mentioned sixteen times.

For a long time, Capernaum was abandoned and even the memory of where it stood was lost. But Capernaum was rediscovered and, in 1894, the Franciscan Custody of the Holy Land acquired the land and continued the excavations of the synagogue and the site of Peter's house, described in the fourth-century testimony of the pilgrim Egeria.

Some years ago, I visited Capernaum with a group of priests. We saw the magnificent ruins of that synagogue built by the centurion whose prayer is repeated in our liturgy, "Lord, I am not worthy that you should enter under my roof." There, in the place where Jesus gives us the eucharistic discourse recorded in chapter 6 of John's Gospel, we read aloud the "I am the bread of life" sermon. There, at that synagogue, where Jesus preached so many times, is probably the very place where Jesus cured Jairus's young daughter, as well as the woman with the hemorrhages and the man with the withered hand.

The Gospels speak to us about Mary going to Capernaum with Jesus after the wedding feast of Cana and describe Jesus's activity at Capernaum, what he did on the lakeshore and in particular what he did in the synagogue and the house of Peter and Andrew.

This house was not only the place where Jesus lived, but it was "a house of formation" for his disciples, a beautiful and eloquent image of the Church. The Evangelist Mark sheds more light on the role of Peter's house in the mystery of the Church. After proclaiming the parables and other teachings to the crowds, Jesus would give a "private teaching" back at Peter's house. The house was often so crowded with disciples it was impossible to enter. Mary and the apostles had to wait outside, and the friends of the paralytic had to open a hole in the roof to get their friend close to Jesus.

I like to think of Peter's house at Capernaum as the field hospital Pope Francis speaks of. The Gospels tell us that the people brought the sick and suffering from miles around to the door of Peter's house.

We celebrated Mass at the site of Peter's house. In the ruins, there is evidence that the early Christians made a "house church" out of this compound where Peter, Andrew, Peter's mother-in-law, and his extended family lived with Jesus. Peter's house was a beehive of apostolic activity: of preaching, of healing, of forming ministers.

At Capernaum, as in our ministry, Jesus also experiences frustration, failure, and disappointment. At one point, Jesus complains that if Sodom and Gomorrah had as much ministry performed there as had been done in Capernaum, those people would have all been converted long ago.

Our expectations, our hope for success, need to be tempered by the conviction that one sows and another reaps. We cannot always have the consolation of the fruit of our labor.

Our Capernaum can be tough. As I always say, being a Catholic in Boston is a contact sport. There can be a lot of heartbreak in Capernaum.

The thirty-year stint in Nazareth begins when Jesus returns to Nazareth after the brief exile in Egypt; I say return because Jesus was conceived in Nazareth at the Annunciation. In the Basilica, the spot is marked by the inscription: *Hic verbum caro factum est* (Here the Word was made flesh).

After the death of Herod, Joseph takes Mary and the Christ Child back to the land of Israel, but hearing that Herod's son Archelaus was ruling over Judea, Joseph, warned in a dream, goes to Galilee to the town of Nazareth so that what had been spoken through the prophet might be fulfilled: "He shall be called a Nazorean." But He could just as easily have been called a "Capharnaumer."

The two poles of Jesus's life are Nazareth and Capernaum. Reflecting on this reality has important implications for our own priesthood.

Three decades of Jesus's short life on earth were lived in Nazareth. These years were an important preface to what followed in his public ministry. We must be convinced that Jesus's long hidden life was not a wasted period, or that he was treading water; it was a crucial part of his sojourn on earth, part of his identity and mission.

In Nazareth, I was pleased to visit the Poor Clare Monastery where Charles de Foucault lived as a gardener and handyman. I asked the nuns for the job and they said I did not qualify. In his homily for the Beatification of Blessed Charles de Foucault, Pope Benedict XVI said that at Nazareth, Blessed Charles discovered the truth about the humanity of Jesus and invites us to contemplate the mystery of the incarnation. Blessed Charles discovered that Jesus, who came to join us in our humanity, invites us to universal brotherhood. As a priest, Blessed Charles placed the Eucharist and the gospel at the heart of his life, for the two tables of the word and of the Bread are the source of Christian life and mission.

At Nazareth, we see Jesus's kenosis, his self-emptying in the incarnation. Jesus is sent by the Father to proclaim good news to the world. The long and hidden years of Nazareth are part of the gospel message. Jesus at Nazareth takes on a poor person's condition and makes ordinary daily life a meeting place with the Father.

Nazareth is the place of Jesus's hidden life, an ordinary life, a place of family life, of prayer, of work, silent virtues, hospitality, friendship, routine, a banal repetition of simple chores and tedious tasks. It is also a place of community in sharing both sorrows and joys. It is a place of a simple lifestyle, of humble service and reciprocal love.

In our lives as priests, we need Nazareth and Capernaum. There is a tension between the two, but it behooves each priest to resolve that tension by embracing both aspects of our priestly vocation.

Jesus spent thirty years in Nazareth and three in Capernaum—ten times longer in Nazareth than in Capernaum. As

Americans, we are very prone to activism and more comfortable in Capernaum, but we need Nazareth if Capernaum is going to work for us.

For a priest, Nazareth is that safe place, the intimacy of being close to a small circle of friends or family who share our faith and ideals. Nazareth is time and space to grow in our relationship with the Eucharist and the word of God. Nazareth is where our intimacy with the Lord allows us to embrace a simple lifestyle and celibacy, to persevere in ministry and confront failure. Nazareth is that oasis of prayer and spirituality without which it is impossible to cross the desert, to carry the treasure to God's people waiting on the other side in Capernaum. Nazareth keeps Christ at the center of our life; his friendship motivates all our activities.

Nazareth is about friendship, personal renewal, study, prayer, growing in self-knowledge, and having a sense of purpose born of our love for the gospel.

Even when he was in Capernaum, Jesus made Nazareth moments in his life: prayer late at night, forty days of retreat in prayer and fasting, and hours in the Garden of Olives.

Without Nazareth, we can spin out of control and drift away from our God and away from our brothers. Without Nazareth, we become too self-absorbed, obsessing about our privacy, our time, our hobbies, our creature comforts we use to compensate for celibacy and other sacrifices inherent in our vocation.

Nazareth can equip us with the deep faith life that gives passion to our ministry. Without Nazareth, Capernaum can become overwhelming, frustrating, and alienating.

Capernaum is the other pole in a priest's life. It is ministry, pastoral love, service, laying down one's life for the sheep. Just as in the gospel, Capernaum is about preaching the gospel and healing the sick. At Capernaum Jesus and the apostles are staying at Peter's house. The paradigm for Church is always family with the in-laws and the outlaws and even the mothers-in-law. Peter's household comes equipped with a mother-in-law who cooked for Jesus.

Capernaum demonstrates Jesus's predilection for the sick and the suffering. A Christ-like priest always sees a special mission to the suffering as a priority in ministry. Our mission is to be messengers of the good news to the poor, and to liberate those oppressed by the circumstances of their lives.

Our pastoral plan must underscore the importance of building communities that are indeed Christ's family. A priest must be a builder of unity in the family of the parish, connecting our people with God and with each other.

Capernaum is also the venue for training people for ministry. The apostles received much of their formation at Peter's house. An important part of our task in Capernaum is to promote priestly vocations as well as lay ministry so that the Church will truly be an evangelizing community, calling people to be evangelizers and disciple makers. The culture of encounter and the art of accompaniment that Pope Francis speaks about so often must characterize our Capernaum experience.

Much of Jesus's vocational recruitment activities centered on the area of Capernaum. It was there that Jesus called Peter, Andrew, James and John, and Matthew. Part of our Capernaum experience of priests must be a constant concern for promoting vocations by challenging our young people to consider a vocation.

A few years ago I went to my home parish to celebrate the seventieth anniversary of the parish. There were forty priests, vocations from the parish, concelebrating the Mass. At our St. Andrew's dinners and vocational retreats it is obvious that some communities are very serious about referring young men yet other parishes never send anyone. Our hope is that the pastoral planning process will help all our people realize how important vocation ministry is for the future of the Church.

For a priest or bishop, inviting young men to consider a priestly vocation must be a pastoral priority. All studies indicate how powerful an invitation is when it comes from a priest. As it was one of Jesus's main focuses at Capernaum, it must be a priority in the Capernaum of daily ministry. It is the way we attend not only to the present pastoral needs of our people, but also the future needs of the community of faith.

Nazareth and Capernaum need to be constants in the life of a priest. As we are living longer, we have another opportunity to spend more time in Nazareth, more time in adoration and prayer so that, like Aaron and Hur, we can help hold Moses's arms aloft. Our prayer allows us to continue to contribute to the faith life of our Church. In the beautiful gospel scene of the Presentation in the Temple, we see Mary with the Baby and Joseph with the birds, but we also see the seniors praying, witnessing, and encouraging.

They are protagonists in the unfolding mission of the Church. Simeon and Anna are a sign of hope and a source of spiritual power in our Church. Many of our retired priests tell me how fervently they are praying for our Church. Their priestly service continues in the Nazareth mode of their ministry. Many of our senior priests whose tireless work built up the parishes and ministries of the Archdiocese are now our prayer warriors whose intercession is a source of strength to our presbyterate and our people, as the center of gravity shifts from Capernaum back to Nazareth in their lives.

To me, Pope Francis's call to embrace the culture of encounter and the art of accompaniment is reflected in the virtue, common to Nazareth and Capernaum, of hospitality. The Holy Father encourages us to be open and welcoming. Pope Francis once spoke of a parish secretary in the Archdiocese of Buenos Aires who was known as the tarantula.

Andrew Greeley, in his book *The Catholic Revolution*, suggested that bishops, priests, and parish staff members ought to have a course from the people who administer the Four Seasons Hotel chain on how to be friendly and attractive to the people they welcome to the sacraments. As it is now, Father Greeley claimed, it often seems that we have been trained by the U.S. Postal Service. (What's wrong with the Postal Service?)

In his pastoral letters where Paul describes the attributes of those who are to be called to ministry, hospitality ranks very high. The epistles are sprinkled with a call to be hospitable. In Hebrews we read, "Let mutual love continue. Do not neglect to show hospitality to strangers, for by doing that some have entertained angels without knowing it" (13:1–2). Certainly, an allusion to Abraham and Sarah, who showed such gracious hospitality to three strangers at an oasis of Mamre.

In the parable of the last judgement, Jesus says, "I was a stranger and you welcomed me" (Matt 25:35). Even those blessed did not know that they were welcoming Jesus in a distressing disguise, to use Mother Teresa's language.

When we invite Christ into our lives, and that is what the hospitality of Nazareth is all about, Christ who is the guest becomes the host, as He did for the disciples on the road to Emmaus.

At the Last Supper, the first Eucharist and ordination are prefaced by the most profound ceremony of hospitality performed by Jesus, who washes the feet of his apostles. Any effort at evangelization will be successful only to the degree that priests and bishops live the spirit of hospitality of Nazareth as well as the hospitality of Peter's house in Capernaum.

The hospitality of the gospel is about welcoming the stranger and, like the Good Samaritan, making the stranger the object of our love, part of our community, even a brother. Gospel hospitality is always disinterested. When you have a banquet, Jesus says, don't just invite rich neighbors and friends who can reciprocate, but invite the poor, the cripple, the lame, and the blind. In inviting them we are inviting Christ and we will be repaid at the resurrection of the righteous.

Hospitality is about building relationships and forming community. In our parishes, hospitality must be contagious, and it should begin with the open welcoming spirit of the clergy who teach more by example and witness than by words.

A great priest once said, "The two happiest questions a priest can hear from someone are 'Father, will you hear my confession?' and 'Father, how can I become a Catholic?'" Whenever you visit a convent of the Missionaries of Charity of Mother Teresa, you will find in the chapel next to the crucifix the words "Sitio," "I thirst." Christ is thirsting for souls. The priest, like the Good Shepherd, is anxious to bring the sheep on the periphery to center stage.

The priest is always a man of hospitality welcoming the prodigal son or daughter, binding up the wounds of the stranger left half dead by the roadside, feeding the hungry with bread, forgiveness, and hope. The hospitality of Nazareth, welcoming Christ, letting the Word become flesh in our hearts is what prepares us for the hospitality of Capernaum, of the field hospital.

We are not alone. Our priesthood unites us to Christ and to one another in a profound and permanent relationship. The ordination ceremony during which the entire presbyterate imposes hands on the newly ordained and then comes forward to give them the kiss of peace is a striking sign of the hospitality we need to practice with each other, looking out for our brothers, encouraging them and helping them. When we renew our priestly vows together, we commit to be part of an intentional presbyterate, a band of brothers committed to living the hospitality of Nazareth and of Capernaum so that the love of the Good Shepherd will be present and visible, especially at the periphery, so that the anointing that we share may reach all of God's people and fill their hearts with hope and joy.

Spelling bees are being relegated to the dustbin of the previrtual age, being surpassed by spell check on the computer, but I still find spelling bees stimulating. Recently, one of the arcane words used in the national spelling bee in Washington was *Capharnaum*.

The definition in the *Webster's Unabridged Dictionary* is "a confused jumble, a place marked by a disorderly accumulation of objects." This is much like the crowd in front of Peter's house in *Capharnaum*.

In the French dictionary, the definition for the word *Capharnaüm* is similar: "L'endroit en desordre...."

I am convinced that our ministry can be *Capharnaum*—a confused and disordered jumble—if the Nazareth values of contemplation, prayer, intimate friendship, the sense of fraternity are lacking. Let us commit ourselves to live with one foot in Nazareth and one foot in *Capharnaum,* to be a priest after the heart of the Good Shepherd.

3

PREACHING

We are anointed to preach the
good news to the poor.

Many times it has been my joy to visit the chapel at the English College in Rome. Many priests who studied at that venerable college lost their lives preaching the gospel during the events of the sixteenth and seventeenth centuries in England. During that time of persecution, whenever an English priest was martyred, usually tortured, drawn, and quartered, the students and the faculty would gather in that same chapel and chant a Te Deum in thanksgiving. They were praising God for the courageous witness and selfless ministry of their former classmates and companions who bravely faced torture and death for their love of Christ and the Church. Our Chrism Masses should be a Te Deum for the ministry of our brothers.

During the Jubilee of the year 2000, St. John Paul II stressed the role of martyrs in the life of the Church. With their suffering they witnessed to the Church's faith in Jesus

Christ crucified and risen. The faith is not spread by pundits or even by teachers, but by teachers who are witnesses. *Martyr* means "witness."

As a young priest, it was a privilege for me to know Oscar Romero, the archbishop of San Salvador. I spent a month with him at Puebla, visited him in San Salvador, and often received the priests whom he sent to me because their lives were in danger. A few days before his death he said, "I have frequently been threatened with death. I must say that as a Christian I do not believe in death, but in the resurrection. Martyrdom is a grace from God that I do not believe I have earned, but you can tell them that if they succeed in killing me that I pardon them, but I wish that they could realize that they are wasting their time. A bishop will die but the Church will never die." On March 24, 1980, Archbishop Romero was murdered while celebrating Mass in a chapel of a Catholic hospital. The Gospel that was read at that Mass is the one where the people are telling Jesus that Pilate has murdered some Galileans and mixed their blood with the blood of the sacrifices that they were offering. Monsignor Romero's blood was mixed with the blood of Christ at the last Mass that he celebrated. He was martyred for preaching the good news to the poor.

Jesus initiates his ministry in a liturgical setting, reading the lesson from the Book of Isaiah, "The spirit of the Lord God is upon me and has anointed me to bring glad tidings to the poor." We recall too that we have been anointed to bring glad tidings to the poor. In a special way we are to be martyrs, witnesses to the resurrection. It is highly unlikely that we shall be called upon to shed our blood like the English martyrs or Oscar Romero, or spend decades in prison like Cardinal Van Thuan, the Vietnamese bishop. The martyrdom that a priest is called to in his ordination, the special witness that we are privileged to give, takes place in the pulpit and in ministry.

In St. John Paul II's letter to close the Jubilee of 2000, *Novo Millennio Ineunte,* he challenged us with the words of the Gospel, *Duc in Altum,* "cast your nets into the deep." "We must rekindle in ourselves the impetus of the beginnings of the Church and allow ourselves to be filled with the ardor of the apostolic preaching which followed Pentecost. We must revive in ourselves the burning conviction of Paul who cried out: 'Woe to me if I do not preach the Gospel'" (no. 40).

St. Fidelis of Sigmaringen, the Capuchin priest who at the time of the Reformation lived in Switzerland and who was martyred while in the pulpit, was the protomartyr of *Propaganda Fide*.

The pulpit is the important arena of our martyrdom, of our witnessing. It can be painful. It can be frustrating. But it can also produce much fruit. Both *Lumen Gentium* and *Presbyterorum Ordinis* state that proclaiming the word of God is the first task, the *Primum Officium* of the ordained priest. The document says that the people of God are joined together primarily by the word of the living God and rightfully they expect this from their priest. Since no one can be saved who does not first believe, priests as coworkers with their bishops have the primary duty, the *Primum Officium,* of proclaiming the gospel of God to all (no. 4).

St. Paul, speaking about the preaching ministry in Romans, writes, "How can they believe if they have not heard and how can people preach unless they are sent?" (10:14–15). As priests and deacons, we are anointed and sent to preach so that God's people can hear his words and hear the assurance that today these words are fulfilled in your hearing. In the Letter to Timothy, Paul writes about presbyters who toil in preaching, in teaching. Today with religious illiteracy at an all-time high, we must toil to preach and to teach. We must preach the word in season and out of season, when convenient and inconvenient.

St. John Paul II, who traveled to the ends of the earth, whose speech at the end of his life was often slurred due to his infirmities, told us that preaching must precede, accompany, and crown the administration of the sacraments to ensure their fruitfulness in faith and life. We must be convinced that the kingdom of God is spread by word of mouth. Jesus says, "He who hears you hears me" (Luke 10:16, NKJV). The same Lord commissions us. Go and preach the gospel to every creature. What you hear whispered, preach it on the housetops. Faith depends on hearing and hearing the word of God. As priests we must be men of The Book, men of the word. The seed is the word of God in the parable. It is keener than the two-edged sword.

There is a song about breaking bread on our knees. We need to break open the word of God on our knees. The great theologian Hans Urs von Balthasar had a wonderful expression in German: *Kniende theologie,* "Theology on one's knees." If our study of the Scripture is too academic, we will forget to let God speak to us in his word. The words of Scripture should reveal God to us, challenge us, grace our lives. As Thomas à Kempis says in *The Imitation of Christ,* "It is better to feel compunction than to be able to define it."

If you ever get to Bethlehem, visit the cave where St. Jerome spent years and years of his life compiling his translation of the Scriptures into Latin, the Vulgate. He studied the word of God as a scholar, but first of all as one seeking the face of God. St. Jerome makes the assertion that ignorance of Scripture is ignorance of Christ. The preacher must be able to say, "What we have seen and heard we proclaim now to you."

Several years ago *Reader's Digest* brought out an abridged version of the Bible. A review in the *Washington Post* began,

"In the beginning was the Word but the Word was too long, so Reader's Digest abridged it." As preachers we need to delve into the whole Scripture in our search for God's face and to hear his word in the liturgy, in the breviary. We learn to pray the Scriptures, to breathe them into our hearts.

Many years ago, I went to see a play about Edith Stein. The writer was a Guatemalan who had received a very prestigious secular prize for the play. In the play the author is constantly switching back and forth between the Nazi headquarters and the Carmelite convent. I immediately noticed that there was something very special about the sisters' speech, about their dialogue. It was poetic. It was so uplifting. Then I realized that practically everything that they were saying were phrases taken from the Psalms. After years of chanting the Offices, the words of the Psalms leapt from their lips in a time of danger and tragedy. Like Jesus on the cross: many of his seven last words are lifted from the Psalms that he prayed over and over again since his childhood. If we learn to pray using the Scriptures, then God's words will be ever in our hearts and on our lips.

Why is preaching so important today? Why is it so difficult? Our present situation makes good preaching both crucial and challenging. To me one of the best metaphors to describe the reality of the Church in the United States and in our western world is the biblical notion of exile.

Exile in the Old Testament is not just a geographical experience. Exile is a spiritual condition of God's people when they find themselves in a hostile, alien environment where the overriding temptation is assimilation. The cultural pull is to accept and conform to a dominant cultural influence that is incongruent with our faith and with our destiny. For today's world the central claims of the faith are increasingly unwelcomed, and they are received, if not with hostility, at best with the yawn of indifference.

Israel survived the exile because God's people resisted the twin temptation—assimilation on one hand, and despair on the other. Today, our challenge is similar. To resist the temptation to conform to the culture of death, to consumerism, hedonism, individualism. The good news needs to be preached with clarity. "No one will follow an uncertain trumpet blast" (1 Cor 14:8). The good news must be preached with a compelling sense of urgency and a profound trust in God and hope in his words.

Some of our people have despaired. They feel that the march of modern culture away from God is inexorable and that we are powerless to influence it. They fall into a grim stoicism of passive resistance and resignation. We must learn to identify the good things as well as the bad in our society and read the signs of the times.

Although we address ourselves first of all to the community of believers, to the exiles in the midst of Babylon, we must realize that the claims of the gospel have a compelling message for the Babylonians as well. They are always overhearing the good news. We must let them hear the liberating news of the gospel in such a way that it touches on public issues, social causes, and the policies that effect the common good.

St. John Paul II's philosophical defense of truth in *Veritatis Splendor* was met with gratitude by many intellectuals outside the Church. The gospel values of human dignity, human freedom, and justice find fertile soil in the secular world, which feels the water of chaos and violence rising around it. The Church's teaching on life and the family are essential for civilization in the long run. We might be living in exile, but we cannot be in a ghetto. From prison, St. Paul reminds us, "The word of God is not chained" (2 Tim 2:9).

In the movie *Contact*, U.S. scientists somewhere in the desert in the Southwest are sending out radio signals to outer space to see if there is any intelligent life out there. Sometimes preaching is like that. We wonder, is anybody listening? The lights are on but is anybody home? Once, visiting a church in Palm Beach I asked the pastor, "How big is your church?" He said, "Bishop, my church sleeps seven hundred."

As a child when we would come home from church, my brothers and I would be quizzed by my Dad about the Sunday Gospel and Father's sermon. If we didn't remember what he talked about, we would say, "Oh, he talked about money, Dad." That would be the end of the discussion. My father did not like that. But Dad was trying to make sure that we learned to listen. In the past, Catholics really did not expect too much from the Sunday sermon. The most important features were its length—it should be short—the jokes, and the baseball scores. The Sunday Mass obligation was fulfilled by arriving for the Offertory. I remember once in Ireland being told by a man who was taking a smoke during the sermon, "Oh, it's all right, Father, as long as you can see someone that can see the priest."

We need to teach our people to listen to the word of God, to listen to the homily. The more importance that we give to the Liturgy of the Word, the more importance our parishioners will give to it. Are the lectors trained, presentable, reverent, focused on the Scripture? How do we prepare and deliver our homilies? Bible courses in our parishes also help prepare our people to listen to the word of God. And, do we share our own faith journey with our people when we speak to them? Prophetic preaching is challenging because it requires a conversion for both preacher and hearers. Both the priest and the people need to be anointed by the Spirit that allows us to desire to hear and to be challenged by the gospel. I have always loved a particular story about John Vianney, who was known as "Curé d'Ars" (the parish priest of Ars). It tells of a few old biddies in the parish who ask the Curé d'Ars to celebrate a Mass every Wednesday morning for their special intentions. The saint did this for many weeks and finally he was a little curious. He said, "Well, apparently you haven't gotten your prayer answered yet. Can you tell me what it is we are praying for?" They said, "Yes, Father, we are praying that the bishop sends you to another parish." A prophet is not without honor except in his own land.

Sometimes we should talk to our parish councils about our preaching. Ask our people what points need to be stressed and what issues raised. What areas of people's lives need to be illumined by the word of God? In the past I have often discussed my pastoral letters with my diocesan pastoral council, and I found it so helpful, so illuminating. Preparing homilies with other priests and deacons can also enrich the content of our reflections and allows the opportunity to witness our faith to each other and strengthen our own proclamation of the good news of Jesus Christ to our people. Are we preaching to the choir? Yes, definitely, but if we touch their hearts then the choir will become the messengers and the inviters. I once heard someone say, "Oh, I don't invite anyone to my parish because its dullsville." When people are excited about the liturgy, they will bring more people to church. They will become evangelizers because we have given them the tools and the motivation.

I have heard many of our priests give eloquent homilies, and we rejoice when we hear one, but we don't want to reduce this ministry to the art of public speaking. St. Paul's most eloquent sermon in Athens at the Areopagus went over like a lead balloon and rendered only paltry results by Paul's standards. Our preaching must be a prayer from our hearts, a burning witness of our faith in Jesus Christ. Like the Greeks in the gospel who went to the apostles and said, "Sir, we wish to see Jesus" (John 12:21). Our people want to see Jesus. We must show them Jesus in our holiness, in our mercy, in our purity, in our prayerfulness.

The real pelican can be a symbol for the preacher. The mythical pelican was supposed to have wounded its breast so that it could feed its flesh to its young and so it has become a eucharistic symbol. But in reality, pelicans consume food first and then, having digested it, offer it to their young. We need to digest the word of God so that we will be able to feed our people.

Father Walter Burkhart, SJ, who at ninety years of age was still climbing onto pulpits, said, "If God does not speak through me, I am a noisy gong, a clanging symbol. For my homily is a prayer in preparation and in the pulpit, I stand before God in praise of Him and not of my own rhetorical perfection because, aware of my weakness I, too, need the Word I preach." The problem is that we are not convinced that preaching must be our priority. Even though the Council and the pope tell us that it is. Even our people tell us that it is the most important role of the priest.

A national opinion research center conducted extensive surveys with the Catholic laity and was forced to conclude that the strongest correlation of church attendance and Catholic identification for both the young people and the general Catholic population were not issues of sex, birth control, abortion, and the ordination of women, rather the strongest predictor of Catholic behavior and identification was the quality of the Sunday sermon preached in the respondent's parish church. In another survey of thirty-year-olds returning to the Church, the two most important factors were a personal relationship with the priest and the quality of preaching. Both of these things underscore the important role of the priest in the life of the Church. The priest is irreplaceable.

The second problem is that we are not always convinced of the power of preaching. Citing the testimonies of the fathers of the Church, Yves Congar said he wished that the following words would be emblazed over every chancery and over every rectory door: "If in one country Mass was celebrated for thirty years without preaching and in another they were preaching without the Mass, the people would be more Christian in the country where there was preaching." I am sure that Congar is not referring to public speaking but a preaching that comes from the heart of priests committed to the path of holiness.

We have only to look at the New Age bookshelves and the psychic hotlines and television stations to see that there is a hunger for God and for spirituality among our people, but today's audience is not easy. The baby boomers born between 1946 and 1966 are seventy-six million Americans, the most educated and affluent group in U.S. history. They are heirs to Woodstock, the drug culture, the sexual revolution, feminism, the breakdown of authority, and divorce. Typically, they are religious illiterates, but they are interested. Not big on dogmas. "My karma ran over my dogma" could be their motto. They are oppressed for time and they are addicted to entertainment. Even the news must be entertaining. They are shaped by the media that teaches them the modern myths and yet they are hungry for God, for spirituality, and for answers about suffering, death, and love, themes found in the bestselling book, *Tuesdays with Morrie*.

Millennials, however, chose spirituality over religion. They are searching but have little patience for institutions and organized religion. Yet, they are open to the message. It is important that we help them see the beauty of the gospel and to experience the love of God so that they do not discard the Church as an old-fashioned club with silly rules.

Leo Trese once said that preaching is the eighth sacrament. It is not for nothing that we must be ordained before we can preach. It is not for nothing that we wear a stole for this sacred function. It is not for nothing that the apostles ordained deacons to feed the poor so that they themselves might have more time for prayer and for the ministry of preaching. My brothers, when we preach, we are handling the word of God, the wisdom of the Father, and the Word is Christ. It is the same Christ we handle in the Eucharist. Here too we must imitate what we handle, become one with Christ whom we handle, lest as St. Paul says, after having preached to others, we be disqualified ourselves (see 1 Cor 9:27).

Let me close with the stirring words of St. John Paul II in *Novo Millennio Ineunte*. "The risen Jesus accompanies us on our way and enables us to recognize Him as the disciples of Emmaus did in the breaking of the bread. May He find us watchful, ready to recognize His face and to run to our brothers and sisters with the good news, we have seen the Lord" (no. 59).

4

FOUR KISSES

When I was studying at Saint Fidelis of Sigmaringen Seminary, there were of course no computers or internet. In fact, there were no televisions or radios and very seldom was a seminarian allowed to make a telephone call. The one concession to modernity was the practice of showing a movie on the eve of big feast days, in part because we would not have to rise at 4:30 the next day. As it turned out, all the movies shown had one thing in common: John Wayne. The Dean was a very strict censor and was not about to let any worldly films corrupt his seminarians. John Wayne films were considered safe and appropriate.

Father Maurice's diligence in screening the films brings to mind the pastor in the movie *Cinema Paradiso*, which takes place in a village in Sicily in the middle of the 1940s. In Italy there are still many communities where the venue for the local cinema is the parish hall and it is under the supervision of the priest. In *Cinema Paradiso*, the pastor would review the films ahead of time, and when he rang a little bell, that was a signal to the projectionist to stop the film and edit out the love scenes, which in those days consisted of a kiss. When the pictures were shown, the parishioners would routinely boo every time one of these spliced and edited scenes would be projected on the screen.

Father Maurice did not have to cut out any scenes, because in John Wayne movies there were no kisses. In contrast to John Wayne, the Catholic priest in the performance of his duties is called upon by the Church to kiss on various significant occasions. I would like to reflect on some of the priests' kisses. There are four kisses of the Catholic priest. The priest kisses the altar. The priest kisses the Gospel. The priest gives a kiss of peace to his people. The priest kisses the cross.

One of the principles of Catholic theology is *lex orandi lex credendi*. Literally: the law of praying is the law of believing. In other words, the liturgy reveals a lot about what we believe. Looking at the kiss in the liturgy helps us to discover those loves that define the heart of a priest.

THE ALTAR

The celebration of Mass always begins with a priest drawing near to kiss the altar. This liturgical custom dates from the first centuries of the Church. In our tradition the altar is a symbol of Christ, who is the rock, the cornerstone on which our Church is built. We describe Christ as being the priest, the victim, and the altar.

Hence, when the priest is about to kiss the altar, he is kissing Christ.

The same gesture is repeated at the conclusion of the Eucharist.

The priest must be the friend of the Bridegroom, as John the Baptist said, "I am not the Messiah, I am but the friend of the Bridegroom" (John 3:28–29). Yes, Jesus is the Bridegroom, never the widower. He does not exist separate from his Bride, the Church. Like John the Baptist, the priest must be the friend of the Bridegroom.

The basis for our ministry in life has to be our friendship with Christ. Kissing the altar cannot be a formalistic or empty gesture. It must betoken our attachment to Christ, our loyalty to him, our friendship.

In the liturgy of St. John Chrysostom before receiving Communion, the priest prays, "Of thy mystic supper receive me today, O Son of God, as a partaker; for I will not speak of the mystery to thine enemies; I will not kiss Thee as did Judas; but as the thief, I will confess Thee, 'Lord, remember me in thy kingdom.'"

Judas's kiss was a lie. It did not betoken friendship and love for Christ, but rather love of power and money. The authentic priestly kiss is one that betokens self-emptying and renunciation for the sake of the Beloved. I always like to say that poverty does not always lead to love. But love always leads to poverty. Our love of Christ must lead us to embrace his kenosis.

Each time we renew our priestly vows, let us be mindful of how these promises can deepen our friendship with Jesus. Our fidelity to prayer and to our commitment to celibacy can draw us closer to Christ, the High Priest and Bridegroom. Ironically enough, in today's world where fewer people are getting married, more people attack the Church's practice of celibacy.

Oftentimes in our culture the avoidance of marriage is based on a will to live for oneself and therefore is a no to the bond of marriage. Celibacy is meant to be the opposite: it is a definitive yes. It is to give oneself into the hands of the Lord. And therefore, it is an act of loyalty and trust, and that also implies the fidelity of marriage. Celibacy is a sign of the presence of God in the world, a reminder that God is to be loved above all else. The pastoral life of the Church has benefited greatly from the generous availability of men and women who have embraced a vocation of celibacy.

I know of a wonderful, faith-filled, young couple who are both doctors and want to be missionaries. They asked me to suggest different missions where they might go to offer their gifts and serve the poor. I put them in touch with bishops in Papua New Guinea and in Paraguay. In the end they came to me and said it would be impossible for them to go to those countries because they want to have children and they worried about Zika. I certainly understand the logic.

When I was in seminary and three of my classmates left for Papua New Guinea, they were told, "You are going to get malaria, dengue, leeches, and fleas. Not necessarily in that order, but you will get them all." I daresay if my classmates had wives and children, they would have had to think long and hard before answering the call to go to Papua New Guinea.

Our celibacy is to make us even more available to love Christ and serve people. Theologically it is meant to be the sign of Jonah, the sign of the resurrection. That we are all called to live forever and therefore it is not necessary for everyone to have children in order to live on in their posterity.

A priest is above all a friend of Christ. Our love for Christ is what draws us to our vocation and allows us to find meaning and purpose in our ministry. We kiss the altar as we approach and we kiss it as we leave, just as a husband kisses his wife when he comes home and kisses her when he leaves.

In the Maronite liturgy there is a beautiful apostrophe the priest addresses to the altar before leaving at the end of Mass. The priest says, "Remain in peace, O holy altar of God. I hope to return to you in peace. May the offering I have received from you forgive me my sins and prepare me to stand blameless before the throne of Christ. I know not whether I shall be able to return to you again to offer sacrifice.

Guard me, O Lord, and protect your Holy Church, that she may be the way to salvation and the light of the world. Amen."

When a Maronite priest dies, his brother priests carry the coffin, walking around the altar praying this prayer of farewell to the altar.

GOSPEL BOOK

The next kiss a priest bestows is after the proclamation of the Gospel. He kisses the word of God as he prays: *Per evangelica dicta deleantur nostra delicta*, "May the reading of the Gospel cleanse me of my sins."

The priest is a man of the gospel. Jesus's words and actions are what must mold the priest's heart so that he may become an icon of the Good Shepherd.

Jesus tells us that he has been anointed to announce the gospel to the poor and the downtrodden. Priests are also anointed to be heralds of the same gospel, ordained to be missionaries on fire with the desire to share the good news with everyone. Christ has called us to be fishers of men and too often we are keepers of the aquarium.

We must meditate on the Gospels frequently so that the words and the inflections of the voice of the Good Shepherd become our own. Our role as preacher and teacher is crucial. We must be constantly preparing for this responsibility by our life of prayer, study, and reflection. Everything a priest does should teach the gospel. Our words, our actions, our attitudes. Being a missionary is born of a constant struggle to deepen our own conversion; so that like the Baptist we can say, I must decrease, he must increase.

KISS OF PEACE

Having kissed the altar and the Gospels, the next kiss is bestowed on the Bride of Christ, the people of God, our brothers and sisters whom we are called to serve. We must love our people and share their life. It is not a matter of being popular, but of being a spiritual father.

In the film *Ryan's Daughter*, there is a touching portrayal of a parish priest, Father Hugh Collins, who demonstrates such concern for his people in an Irish village during the uprising. His constant companion is a man who has an intellectual disability, Michael. When the village rises up against Rosy Ryan, accusing her of being a collaborator with the British, they beat her and cut off her hair. It is her pastor who protects and consoles her. As priests we need to have a special love for those on the margins, on the periphery, as Pope Francis is wont to say.

We need to love our people and help them find meaning in life, to discover their purpose and embrace their mission. We must emulate the Curé d'Ars who used to pray to the Lord, "Grant me the conversion of my parish, and I accept to suffer all you wish for the rest of my life." St. John Vianney did everything he could to pull people away from their own lukewarm attitude in order to lead them back to love.

The Kiss of Peace is part of the liturgy from the earliest centuries and is a stark reminder that we are priests not for ourselves, but for our people. We must love them as the Good Shepherd who lays down his life. It is only when they know that we love them that they are willing to listen to us and accept our message.

Yes, even the message of the gospel can be rejected because of the messenger who does not know how to communicate the gospel with love, with a kiss.

THE CROSS

We live in a culture that sees pain and suffering as the greatest evil. We are often like Peter, who tries to keep Jesus from even talking about the cross. Jesus rebukes St. Peter, "Get behind me, Satan! You are a stumbling block to me; for you are setting your mind not on divine things but on human things" (Matt 16:23). Also like Peter, we often flee from Gethsemane and Calvary.

The last kiss is at the veneration of the cross, which is part of the Good Friday service. To savor the cross is to savor the things of God. At our ordinations we all receive the chalice and paten as the bishop says, "Understand what you do, imitate what you celebrate, and conform your life to the mystery of the Lord's cross."

On the cross, Jesus is offering himself with the very compassion that transforms the suffering of the world into a cry to the Father. We must learn to accept more profoundly the sufferings of pastoral life, which is entering into the mystery of Christ. Rejection of the cross breeds mediocrity.

On Good Friday the bishop and priests are invited to kiss the cross first, to give our people an example of faithful discipleship that takes up the cross each day to follow Christ our Master.

I am also mindful that when a man is installed as a bishop, the first thing the Church demands of him is to kiss the cross. Indeed, when I think of my own installation, everything is kind of a blur. On that fateful day, I entered the church, passing through a phalanx of angry demonstrators and aggressive camera men. Then, following the ancient ritual, I banged on the door with the crosier and stepped into a packed cathedral. I was in a daze. However, I can still hear plainly the voice of the master of ceremonies, trying to rouse me from a state of stupor, saying in a stage whisper, "Kiss the cross!"

Outside there was so much negativity and anger, but inside, the people were applauding. The love and faith of the people gave me the courage to kiss the cross.

Jesus didn't suffer and die so that we wouldn't have to. He suffered and died in order to endow our sufferings with the redemptive value, something they would never possess on their own. He suffered and died in order to invest his love with us. He did this so that our love, while not diminishing our suffering or sparing us from pain, will transform pain into holy passion, suffering into sacrifice.

Yet it is not the magnitude of Christ's suffering that saved us, but rather the magnitude of his love. Love turned his suffering into an offering at the Last Supper, and that love is the Eucharist. It is the Eucharist that transforms Calvary into a sacrifice rather than merely an execution. There the cross of Jesus turned death upside down. Death is the moment we usually associate with loss of life, but Jesus made it the occasion of giving life. Jesus gave his life freely and fully. He transformed it into a gift, a prayer, and a sacrifice.

As we continue to kiss the altar, the Gospel, the people of God, and the cross, let us not allow our kisses to be routine or perfunctory, but rather let our kiss be a striking gesture of the profound loves that define us as Catholic priests.

5

THE PRIORITIES OF JESUS

On one of my birthdays my cousins gave me a Fitbit. I had no idea what it was. After opening the package, I stared at the thing and thought, "If only I can figure out what it is...I can regift it." But when I discovered what the "it" did, I realized that I actually really did need it myself. I suppose my life is typical of most bishops who spend too much time seated in a chair; indeed, the word *cathedral* comes from the word for *chair*. We lead a very sedentary lifestyle. Even to go short distances we tend to go by car to save time.

Recent studies indicate that being in a seated position for hours at a time is not good for our health. The Fitbit counts our footsteps, how many staircases we climb, and how many hours of sleep we get each night. It helps me to set healthy goals: ten thousand steps and seven hours of sleep. I seldom reach those objectives, but I am getting better and I believe it helps contribute to my youthful appearance and boundless energy...well, somewhat.

To lead a healthy lifestyle, we need to have a plan, a Fitbit, something that will help us to follow a healthy regime.

This extends to exercise and healthy eating habits. I have the great sadness of having already buried two of my closest friends. Father Paul was two years ahead of me in the seminary. He was a missionary in Puerto Rico. He was also a "martyr of the table." Despite his diabetes he ate all the wrong things and in industrial size portions. He dropped dead at fifty-five.

The second friend, Father Lorenzo Albacete, was the head of Communion and Liberation in the United States. He was a close friend of St. John Paul II and Father Giussani. He was sought after to appear in television talk shows, as a lecturer, and as a retreat master. He was a scientist by training and worked at NASA before going to the seminary. Lorenzo was also a brilliant theologian and had a capacity to reach young people. He was a rock star, but he was also the poster boy for what chain smoking and an Olympic sedentary life can do. When I would invite Lorenzo to the March for Life, he would say I am going to the "drive for life."

The funerals for both of these priests attracted thousands of mourners deeply moved by their extraordinary ministry, fascinating personalities, and their many gifts and talents. They died too young because they did not have a Fitbit, a plan for a healthy lifestyle, and hence, they deprived God's people of many years of truly great ministry.

I am not going to teach you how to do power walks, jog, or to become vegans. But I do advise you to take time to take stock of your life. Each of us must try to recommit ourselves to a rule of life that brings balance and discipline to our lives.

In addition to developing healthy habits, we want to map out a plan for a spiritual journey that will draw us near to God and help us to be icons of the Good Shepherd.

As part of our own reflection it is always helpful to look to Christ as our model. After all we are his disciples. He is the Master and we are called to follow him, to imitate him. One of the most read spiritual classics is Thomas à Kempis's *The Imitation of Christ*.

In *Gaudete et Exsultate,* Pope Francis speaks to us about following Christ, especially in living the Beatitudes from the Sermon on the Mount and the passage on the works of mercy in Matthew's parable of the last judgement. This parable gives us the great criterion by which we shall be judged. "I was hungry and you gave me food...I was a stranger..." an immigrant, homeless, sick, in prison and you came to my aid (see Matt 25:31–46).

This text from Matthew is not just a simple invitation to charity; it is a page of Christology that sheds a ray of light on the mystery of Christ. In this call to see him in the poor and suffering, we see revealed the very heart of Christ, his deep feelings and choices, his identification with suffering humanity.

Developing a plan for a rule of life is not easy, but it is urgent. In the document of Vatican II *Presbyterorum Ordinis,* we read about the need for unity and integration, balance in our life:

> In the world today, when people are so burdened with duties and their problems, which oftentimes have to be solved with great haste, range through so many fields, there is considerable danger of dissipating their energy. Priests [and bishops], too, involved and constrained by so many obligations of their office, certainly have reason to wonder how they can coordinate and balance their interior life with feverish outward activity. Neither the mere external performance of the works of the ministry, nor the exclusive engagement in pious devotion, although very helpful, can bring about this necessary coordination. [We] can arrive at this only by following the

> example of Christ our Lord in [our] ministry. His food was to follow the will of him who had sent him to accomplish his work. (no. 14)

As bishops and priests, we have so many demands on our time and energy. It is a challenge to balance prayer and action, theory and praxis, feelings and words.

We need a unifying inspiration to help us organize our life and set priorities. Of course, that inspiration, as Pope Francis says, must be centered on Christ. As we examine our own lives and priorities, it can be helpful to meditate on what Jesus's priorities were during his years of public ministry.

A fascinating study was done by the Jesuit Scripture scholar and bishop Cardinal Carlo Maria Martini. I always say that the Capuchins only have a cup of coffee named after us. For the Jesuits there are thirty-six craters on the moon and a cocktail with an olive.

Studying how Jesus organizes his time and activities, Cardinal Martini distilled from a close reading of the four Gospels what seem to be Jesus's five priorities. I would like to share those priorities in a very synthetic way as we consider what our own priorities should be and how they might be reflected in a personal rule of life.

I must confess that I was surprised by the first priority. If I had been asked to give a spontaneous opinion, I would have said that preaching the gospel would have been Jesus's number one priority. However, Martini's analysis shows that Jesus's first priority was his attention to the sick. Jesus dedicated much time to the sick and suffering. Jesus never refuses to draw near and heal anyone for lack of time. So many episodes in the Gospels have as the protagonist people afflicted with various maladies and we are told about Jesus's behavior toward the suffering. To these works of mercy, we can add Jesus feeding the hungry and forgiving sinners.

Mercy is the number one priority. Indeed, mercy is the context in which the gospel can be preached. If people are not convinced that we care about them, they will never believe our preaching. In this first priority we can include what Pope Francis calls *vicinanza*, closeness to the sick, the poor, the marginalized.

The second priority indeed is preaching the gospel, announcing the kingdom of God. In Mark we read, "Now after John was arrested, Jesus came to Galilee, proclaiming the good news of God, and saying, 'The time is fulfilled, and the kingdom of God has come near; repent, and believe in the good news'" (Mark 1:14–15).

The third priority is the meetings, encounters, dialogues, and conversations that Jesus has with the people who listen to and follow him. Jesus seems to give special importance to this direct contact with the people. We even find Jesus "eating with publicans and sinners" because it is the sick who need the physician. "I have come to call not the righteous but sinners," Jesus declares (Luke 5:32).

The fourth priority is prayer. The Gospels show how Jesus dedicated extended periods of time to prayer. Mark says Jesus rose early to pray. He chose solitary places like the Garden of Olives, the desert, the mountaintop. He sometimes spent the whole night in prayer. He prayed intensely in preparation for important occasions, like choosing his apostles, or preparing for his mission, or to ready himself for his death. Jesus participates in the liturgical life of his people. He prays alone, in secret, he prays with his apostles. He prays and he is a teacher of prayer.

The fifth priority is the time Jesus gives to his friends. First of all, in the time he gives to the formation of his apostles and disciples whom he considers "his friends." There is also the time he spends with friends at Peter's house and at Bethany with Lazarus, Martha, and Mary.

I am sure that for Jesus just as for us, friendship is life-giving. It allows us to be people who know how to love and to know that we are loved. Jesus's first healing is Peter's mother-in-law, who often cooked for Jesus, and one of his greatest miracles is raising his dear friend Lazarus from the grave. "See how he loved him!" (John 11:36). The gospel seems to indicate that Jesus went to Bethany to relax, to renew himself with the good food and good conversation that he enjoyed there.

Setting our own priorities and formulating a rule of life can bring focus and unity into our life and ministry. Luke's Gospel describes the famous scene of Jesus at Bethany on one of his visits. Martha preparing a fantastic meal with all of Jesus's favorite dishes, but she is angry, frustrated, and ready to "go into orbit." Jesus tells Martha not to be upset about so many things when only one thing is necessary.

Oftentimes we act like Martha, we have so many demands on our time and attention it leaves us stressed and exhausted. We must focus on the *unum necessarium,* that unity in our lives that will unite us to the mission of the Church and unite us in the life of the Trinity.

I have always liked the gospel story describing how Jesus is preaching and is interrupted by the arrival of a distraught father who asks for help for his daughter who is gravely ill. Jesus drops everything to go with the poor man. Then there is a second interruption when the woman with the hemorrhage stops Jesus and asks for his help. St. Luke does not indicate that Jesus was stressed out by the constant interruption, but continued on his way doing the will of the Father in a life with great unity of purpose and fidelity to mission.

I imagine that many of you have a rule of life. If you do, it's always good to take a moment from time to time to review and update it. If you have no rule of life, now is the time to develop one to achieve greater balance and unity in your life and ministry. I certainly think that the priorities that we find in the gospel are the ideals that inform our own plan of life.

Once you have a game plan, a rule of life is like having a spiritual Fitbit. Then we need to wear it, to count our steps and see if we are moving forward. As the Germans say, *Still-standen ist ruckstritt,* "standing still is going backward."

We can also begin to see if our steps are all in the same direction, if there is a unity and purpose inspired by our love for Jesus and our desire to follow him as *Presbyterorum Ordinis* tells us, "In order to measure and verify this coordination of life in a concrete way, let priests examine all their works and projects to see what is the will of God—namely, to see how their endeavors compare with the goals of the Gospel mission of the Church. Fidelity to Christ cannot be separated from faithfulness to His Church. Pastoral charity requires that priests avoid operating in a vacuum and that they work in a strong bond of union with their bishops and brother priests. If this be their program, priests will find the coordination and unity of their own life in the oneness of the Church's mission" (no. 14).

6

PROTECTING THE CHILDREN

When I became a Capuchin brother, so many years ago, I thought I would be sent to work in one of the missions served by the Capuchin Friars. During my seminary years, St. John XXIII, who was pope at the time, asked that one-fifth of the priests in Canada and the United States would go to help the church in Latin America. That inspired me to learn Spanish, and shortly after I was ordained a deacon, Father General wrote to our Provincial saying that he wanted me to go to Easter Island after my priesthood ordination where I would work with the German Friar who had been there by himself for forty years. Easter Island is one of the most remote inhabited islands in the world. The nearest inhabited island is Pitcairn Island, which is almost 2,000 miles away, and the nearest continental point lies in central Chile about 2,500 miles away. Easter Island belongs to Chile and has about seven thousand inhabitants, mostly Rapa Nui people. The island is best known for the thousand huge stone heads that the natives erected twelve hundred years ago.

I began to study Rapa Nui, the language spoken there with Spanish. I was very excited about the prospect of going to such a challenging mission. However, on the eve of my priesthood ordination, the Cardinal Archbishop of Washington, Patrick O'Boyle, called my superior to say that Latin American immigrants were arriving by the thousands every month to Washington, fleeing the wars in Central America. He told the Provincial that he only had one priest that spoke Spanish and therefore asked that Brother Seán be left in Washington to work with the growing Hispanic population. Hence, I always say I did not go to the missions, the missions came to me. I worked there for twenty years at Centro Católico Hispano in Washington. It was in those years that I started the Portuguese parish that served mostly *retornados*, Portuguese immigrants returning from Portuguese Africa after the Revolution.

Those twenty years of working with Spanish- and Portuguese-speaking immigrants in Washington was the honeymoon of my priesthood and an unmitigated joy. I was having too much fun so God, with his sense of humor, made me a bishop. My first diocese was the Virgin Islands, what had been the Danish West Indies. When I was told that I was going there, I was shocked because I had never been there and so I asked the priest who knew the islands what they were like. He mischievously said, "The Virgin Islands are like the Canary Islands, no canaries." Once again it was an extraordinary pastoral experience working with the Afro-Caribbean people, who have such a deep faith and rich culture. I came to love the Virgin Islands very much.

Up to that point in my life, I had never heard the word *pedophilia*, but in 1992, I was named bishop of Fall River, Massachusetts, also known as the tenth island of the Azores. I was sent there at a time when a terrible scandal developed because a priest, Father James Porter, a serial pedophile, had abused and raped hundreds of children.

Shortly after I arrived, I arranged to have a meeting with victims and their families. I am so grateful that I had that opportunity to hear personally from the individuals and families that had been devastated by clerical sexual abuse. It was amazing to me that for so long this problem was hidden. As painful as the media attention centering on clerical sexual abuse was, it actually did a great service to us in the Church. It forced us to recognize our crimes and sins that caused so much harm to children and vulnerable people.

Part of the problem was that Church leadership and people in society in general had no idea how much harm was done to children who were sexually abused, and particularly when the abuse was a horrendous betrayal by a man who represented God for that child. We know now that many of those children eventually committed suicide, many suffered severe mental illness and depression, and they often fell into terrible addictions. In many cases their entire life was adversely affected. I am convinced that if people in the Church in those days had even suspected how much damage was being done to children they would not have perpetuated the cover-ups and would have immediately removed perpetrators from ministry.

Unfortunately, for a long time bishops and religious superiors did not know how to deal with accusations of abuse and often improvised. It is an issue that has so many dimensions: the victims, the accused, the parish, the presbyterate, as well as the police and judicial authorities. Because there are so many aspects involved, if someone is improvising, they will commit serious mistakes. It is crucial to have a clear, well-developed, and announced policy for child protection. The policy must enunciate the Church's clear commitment to the safeguarding of children as one of our most sacred duties.

After ten years in Fall River, where we worked very hard with our priests and people to develop sound policies for the protection of children, I believe a lot of healing was achieved. Just when I naively thought that the crisis was behind us, I was named to my third diocese, Palm Beach, Florida. There, I was to replace two bishops who had been removed for sexual abuse of minors. At the press conference announcing my nomination as bishop, the first question I received from a journalist was, "Are you a pedophile too?"

After a short tenure of less than a year in Palm Beach, I was gathered with my family who were celebrating my birthday. The phone rang and it was the nuncio who told me that the Holy Father wanted me to go to Boston to replace Cardinal Law. Unfortunately, I did not have "caller ID" on my phone. I would have been tempted not to answer that call.

The situation in Boston was grave. If you have not seen the film *Spotlight*, I would encourage you to do so. It is not easy to watch, so much pain, so much shame; but it was the beginning of the road to conversion, to penance, and to the firm purpose of amendment. People who had suffered for years in silence came forward. It was discovered that priests who abuse children were moved from one parish to another. Our priests and people were all very demoralized. Many turned their back on the faith and left the Church, so great was their anger and disappointment.

When I arrived, the archdiocese was in economic freefall. The situation threatened the existence of Catholic schools, parishes, and apostolates. The archdiocese had an annual operational deficit of $15 million. We owed $35 million to the Knights of Columbus. The Catholic hospitals were losing $40 million per year. The pension fund for our lay employees was failing, and the pension fund for the clergy was bankrupt. In addition, there were a thousand lawsuits against the diocese for cases of clerical sexual abuse. I told my priest counsel that in my first diocese in the West Indies, the entire diocesan budget was $30,000 a year, but I did not owe anyone anything.

At the same time I came to Boston, the crisis was beginning to explode across the country and the Bishops' Conference, under the very capable leadership of Archbishop Wilton Gregory, responded by developing national policies that give priority to the safeguarding of children and care for victims, and that initiated strict protocols of reporting crimes to civil authorities, removing abusers from ministry, screening church personnel and volunteers, training church leadership and parishioners in the principles of safeguarding, and careful attention to seminary recruitment and human formation.

It was a very challenging time for everyone in the Church, but the efforts to develop carefully thought-out protocols that have been embraced and implemented by all the dioceses has resulted in a huge drop in the number of cases. In Boston our last case was in 2006. Some dioceses have not had a single case since 2003. This goes to show that if the bishops do not improvise but rather have a well-thought-out strategy for child protection, it will make a huge difference. I am reminded of the old saying, "An ounce of prevention is worth a pound of cure."

Part of our task as good shepherds is to protect the most vulnerable in our flock, the little children. The Gospel accounts show that our Blessed Savior often uses strong images to draw our attention and to underscore the seriousness of his message. He tells us to pluck out the eye that causes us to sin, to cut off the hand that causes us to fall. Jesus also says that if a person scandalizes a child, it would be better to have a millstone hung around their neck and be thrown into the depths of the sea.

Obviously, Jesus does not want us to adopt this kind of drastic and cruel punishment, but he wants to get our attention, and make us understand the great harm that is caused by scandalizing a child.

The most serious aspect of the scandal of the sexual abuse by clergy is the harm, both spiritual and psychological, caused not only to children and young people who are sexually exploited, but also to their families, friends, and acquaintances, as well as the parish community.

I was baptized by my uncle, a parish priest. I started helping at Mass when I was six and went to the seminary at thirteen. All of my teachers and mentors were priests or religious. They were good and holy people who only gave me good examples and nurtured my faith. But I ask myself, if I had been the victim of a pedophile priest, would I be here today? Would I still be Catholic? Would I have committed suicide like so many?

The fact that many priests abused children is shocking enough, but in the United States many thousands of Catholics also left the Church for another reason, disgusted not only by the sick behavior and human weakness of priests, but also because of the neglect and incompetence of bishops and religious superiors who failed in their task of protecting children against these predators.

Our response as a Church to the sexual abuse of minors must also acknowledge the fact that the number of children all over the world who are suffering one form or another of sexual abuse is beyond imaginable. Secular authorities estimate that one in four girls, and one in seven or eight boys, are sexually abused before the age of eighteen.

Unfortunately, many members of the clergy and many laypeople in the universal Church are convinced that the sexual abuse crisis is an American phenomenon. In today's world of instant communication, Catholics are becoming more aware of the problem of abuse in the Church and throughout the world. It is not a problem circumscribed to certain areas: it is a human problem affecting us all.

However, the sexual abuse crisis certainly affects the Church in a very concrete way. First, it is a stain on the soul of the guilty. In addition, however, it has debased and thrown suspicion over all the good and holy people of the Church, and in particular those who work daily to improve the lives of children and young people around the world.

The entire Church must be united in its commitment to ensure that every parish, school, and agency are safe for children. It is crucial that we follow appropriate standards and procedures for the protection of minors.

The lack of adherence to established rules and procedures has caused great suffering to the victims and their families, great damage to the reputation of clergy and religious, and many have lost confidence in the Church and have even started to question their own faith.

Today, after so many years of pain and suffering, we know that there is no excuse to fail in acting swiftly and decisively in the face of situations of sexual abuse. Pope Francis, continuing the initiatives promoted by Pope Benedict XVI and St. John Paul II, demonstrated on many occasions his commitment, pointing out the errors of the past and expelling from ministry priests and religious who have abused children and young people.

I am very grateful that Pope Francis gathered the presidents of the Episcopal Conferences of the entire world for the important meeting of February 2019. The purpose of the meeting was to help the Church hierarchy understand how very important the protection of minors is, and that, although this is a grave human problem, in the Church we have an even greater and more serious obligation to promote protection.

I hope that one outcome of this work will be the annual evaluation or audit to measure the state of implementation of safeguarding policies by each Episcopal Conference. As difficult as this area of safeguarding is, nothing is more important than to take care of our precious children and to restore faith in the heart of those who have been shocked by the totally inappropriate way the Church handled clerical sexual abuse in the past.

Many people still say they do not agree with the rules of transparency and zero tolerance. As Church leaders we must confront these attitudes. All our action should be motivated by the gospel of Jesus Christ. It is necessary that we behave with courage, removing the guilty from ministry and caring for victims when abuse has been committed.

I would like to reaffirm that the greatest challenge for the Church today is to ensure transparency, accountability, and zero tolerance. If these challenges are not achieved, if we have no firm commitment to these principles, the Church will not be able to restore the confidence of Catholics whose faith has been put to the test.

Unfortunately, we know that one result of this crisis is that millions of faithful have stopped going to Mass and that many charitable and educational institutions of the Church have had to close. I learned recently of a truly amazing fact: in Australia, of all the cases of abuse reported to the Royal Commission, 40 percent occurred in a context linked to our Catholic institutions.

This global crisis has had as a consequence the silencing of the prophetic voice of the Church. In large part this is the result of the perception that Church leadership has not been made accountable and hence has lost people's trust.

We must do all that is in our power to restore the Church's voice in defense of the oppressed and in defense of life. God's people and society have to be able to see that we are absolutely committed to preventing the sexual abuse of children and vulnerable adults and that we respond promptly to all cases of abuse.

Child abuse appears and develops in an atmosphere of secrecy and concealment. The Church has to be the leader in denouncing this serious human problem. Therefore, we have to say clearly that no clergy or religious who has abused a child will be allowed to continue in ministry.

Truly, today, the Church has the opportunity to create a safe environment for children and vulnerable adults. Many other Christian churches and congregations from other religions are interested in learning from the Church's experience and adopting our procedures.

Out of the shame and pain of our recent history, God can bring something good: a Church and a society that put the protection of children among the highest priorities. It is necessary to strive to deserve the trust of the people we serve and also to offer the possibility of returning to those who have left us.

To achieve these goals, we have to be clearly a people, always and everywhere, committed to the safety of the children entrusted to our pastoral care. Only that can heal our Church and restore trust in our pastoral ministry.

7

THE SUFFERING SERVANT

There are one hundred Jesuit priests living in St. Mary's Hall, the Jesuits' residence at Boston College. It must be one of the largest religious houses in the world. I call Father Paul Harmon, who is in charge, the Father Abbott, though not many abbots have that many monks. Father Harmon has one hundred Jesuits waiting on him hand and foot. With three hundred Jesuits in Boston, I have more Jesuits than the Holy Father in the Vatican and I always say when they're good, they're very good.

For a while the largest community of priests in modern time was the Priesterblock. It was the priest section of the concentration camp at Dachau. A cardinal, bishops, and about three thousand Catholic priests were there, in addition to some one hundred Protestant clergy and thirty Orthodox priests. Many did not survive the ordeal. In 1975, I participated in a Mass in St. Peter's with Cardinal Wright and several hundred priests who were survivors of concentration camps. It was one of the most moving experiences of my life. Cardinal Wright often cited the sociological studies done about the concentration camps. The researchers interviewed survivors: Jews, intellectuals, political prisoners, from Italy, France, Germany, Hungary, Poland. All were asked these questions: In the midst of the hell that was the concentration camp, surrounded by all the horror rife in those prisons, horrors that depersonalized, destroyed personality and sanity as well as health, which group remained sane the longest? Which group remained useful the longest? Which group retained its sense of identity the longest? Which people were the last to suffer the crisis about why they were alive, or who they were or what was their task? Which group, nationality, profession, race was most able to forget themselves and their problems so they could serve the others who had the same problems? The answer was almost invariably, Catholic priests.

One of the inmates of the Priesterblock at Dachau was a priest from Luxembourg who kept a diary documenting the torture of the priests. The Nazis crucified priests and crowned them with barbed wire. In 2004, a German film director got a hold of the diary and produced a film called *Der Neunte Tag* (The Ninth Day). The protagonist is a Luxembourg priest, Abbe Kremer, who had been imprisoned for being part of the resistance movement in his country.

One of the most powerful scenes in the film is the Mass the emaciated priests celebrate clandestinely using a crust of bread. Abbe Kremer is promised his freedom if he will cooperate with the Nazis. There are very tense conversations with an SS, Officer Gebhardt, who had been in the seminary but had long since renounced his faith. At one point Gebhardt says, "It was my mother's fondest wish that I become a priest, so as to have a dignitary in the family." Father Kremer answers, "Priests are servants, not dignitaries. My mother knew that."

I was very struck by that phrase because many people do consider the priest a dignitary. The increasing role of the laity, the fallout of the sexual abuse scandal, the secularization of the culture have all caused people to see the priest differently. Yet many still think of priests as dignitaries. All the same, Abbe Kremer and his mother, Madame Kremer, knew that the priest is not a dignitary but is a servant like Jesus is a servant. The more we understand Jesus's identity, the more we will understand our own.

Luke's Gospel details the beginning of Jesus's ministry. This periscope is prefaced with the phrase "He began to teach" (4:14)—this is the way Christ's ministry begins. The account of Jesus's first sermon in the synagogue opens with Jesus choosing the text of Isaiah. For Jesus nothing is improvised, nothing is a coincidence. Isaiah is the great prophet of the Messiah. He speaks of the Virgin who will conceive a son, Emmanuel, God with us. Isaiah describes for us the suffering servant. When people read Isaiah 53 without knowing which part of the Bible it comes from, they often wrongly assume it is from the New Testament. One author claims there are 121 passages in Isaiah that describe Jesus. Isaiah speaks of the servant who is anointed—the Christos, the Messiah—by the Spirit. He goes on to describe Christ's mission; to announce the good news to the poor, restore sight to the blind, to free the captive and the oppressed, to declare a Jubilee. And just to make sure that we did not miss the point, Jesus says, "Today this Scripture has been fulfilled in your hearing" (Luke 4:21). Jesus is the Messiah, the Suffering Servant, the Wounded Healer.

This is the same Christ of whom John writes in the Book of Revelation, "He loves us, He has freed us from our sins, He has made us priests" (1:5–6). He has made us priests because he loves us, not because we are good-looking, clever, or holy, but because he loves us. John goes on to say, "Look! He is coming with the clouds; every eye will see him, even those who pierced him" (1:7). We behold the one who was pierced. The risen Lord is still the Suffering Servant, still the wounded Christ. That is why the risen Lord is so quick to show his wounded hands when he appears to the first priests and says, "Receive the Holy Spirit. If you forgive the sins of any, they are forgiven them" (John 20:22–23). This Suffering Servant loves us and is patient with us: "A bruised reed he will not break, and a dimly burning wick he will not quench" (Isa 42:3).

The fourth chapter of Luke's Gospel depicts for us the inauguration of Jesus's public ministry. Placing this scene first is an important interpretive move, for it suggests that the rest of the Lukan story (the Acts as well as the Gospel) should be read in light of this scene. By citing the Prophet Isaiah, Jesus is providing us an interpretation of his ministry. The descent of the Spirit is an anointing for office. Anointed with the Spirit, Jesus is the Messiah, the Christos, the King of Israel, but his immediate function is prophetic: he is to be the bearer of the good news.

In Luke especially we see the poor as the protagonists of the Gospel. The Suffering Servant is close to those who are poor, marginalized, sick, and forgotten. When Jesus speaks about "the release of captives," this can also refer to Jesus's ministry of reconciliation, the forgiveness of sins. Recovery of sight to the blind refers not only to Jesus's healing power but also to his teaching role that helps people to understand revelation and to see by the light of faith. It is as though Isaiah has written the job description for the Messiah, the Suffering Servant.

When Jesus called his apostles in the Gospel, he said, "Follow me." He didn't say, "How would you like to be suffering servants?" That would be like the Irish marriage proposal, "How would you like to be buried with my people?" But when the apostles were still thinking they were going to be dignitaries, two of them went with their mother to ask for thrones at Jesus's left and right. Jesus responds by asking that terrible question, "Are you able to drink the cup that I am about to drink?" They responded, "We are able" (Matt 20:22). I am sure they had no idea what they were saying.

When we were ordained, the ceremony began with an invitation, "Let those who are to be ordained come forward." We responded blithely, "*Adsum*—Present!" Did we have any idea what we were saying? Like the apostles, we answered with naive enthusiasm. Like a young man making his marriage vows; for better, for worse, for richer, for poorer, in sickness and in health, all the while looking forward to the better, the richer, the good health.

Can you drink of the chalice of the Suffering Servant by whose stripes we are healed? Like the sons of Zebedee, we said, "*Adsum, possumus*, we can." We had no way of knowing that we were being called to be priests in the most challenging time in the history of the Church in our country. Looking back on my days in the West Indies when a hurricane flattened most of our churches, schools, and rectories, I recall that we survived on coconut milk and peanut butter and were without water, phones, or electricity for six months, a year without television (that was a blessing). What could be worse than this, I thought at that time. Having experienced our recent crisis, I say, "Give me a good hurricane any day!"

None of us knew what we were getting into when Christ said, "Follow me." We had only a vague notion that the path might lead to Calvary. We knew in theory. Living it is different.

It is not by accident that one of the symbols of the Catholic priesthood is the chalice. I always felt a little sad that as a Capuchin I could not have my own chalice. I would like to have taken my uncle's, Father Jerry Reidy, the diocesan priest who baptized me, or have a replica of the O'Malley chalice that is in the museum in Dublin. But the chalice is not a trophy. In the national ordination ceremony, the bishop handed us the chalice and paten and said, "Receive the oblation of the holy people to be offered to God. Understand what you do, imitate what you celebrate, conform your life to the mystery of the Lord's Cross." *Agnoscite quod agitis, imitamini quod tractatis*.

The fear of the cross is what makes us mediocre. The fear of suffering. When Jesus prayed, "Let this cup pass from me; yet not what I want but what you want" (Matt 26:39), Peter was watching and listening, but when the soldiers came, the apostles fled, even the ones who said, "We can drink of the cup." They ran. Peter tried to follow Jesus at a safe distance. That didn't work. In the attempt, he denied his master three times. It is impossible to follow Jesus at a safe distance. We need to follow him up close. Later, the risen Christ will ask Peter, and all his priests, "Do you love me?" "Yes, Lord; you know that I love you." "Feed my sheep" (John 21:15–17). A few weeks after that conversation, St. Luke depicts the apostles, including Peter, who have been flogged and beaten for their preaching, for feeding the sheep. They were told not to speak about Jesus and were dismissed. "As they left the council, they rejoiced that they were considered worthy to suffer dishonor for the sake of the name [of Jesus]. And every day in the temple and at home they did not cease to teach and proclaim Jesus as the Messiah" (Acts 5:41–42). They drank from the chalice of suffering and fed the flock of Christ.

We are afraid of the cross. Especially during Lent, praying the Stations, I always identify with Simon of Cyrene. He was pressed into service. He was embarrassed to be part of an execution, angry because he was innocent and forced to be part of a spectacle. He was afraid of what damage would be done to his standing in the community, in his family. I like to think that later Simon of Cyrene looked back on that horrific experience of carrying Christ's cross up Mount Calvary through a hostile crowd as the defining moment in his life. His sons, Rufus and Alexander, surface in Acts and Mark and the Epistles. He must have embraced the faith and passed it on to his family. Still, his hesitancy contrasts with the spontaneous and courageous gesture of compassion of Veronica. She overcame fear and drew near to Christ.

As priests we must overcome our fears: of suffering, of failure, of shame, of sickness, of death, of being alone. Only love can cast out all these fears. Today the High Priest, Good Shepherd, and Suffering Servant offers us the cup to drink. Father Henri Nouwen said, "Drinking the cup that Jesus drinks is living a life in and with the spirit of Jesus which is the spirit of unconditional love. The intimacy between Jesus and Abba, His Father, is an intimacy of complete trust, in which there are no power games, no mutually agreed upon promises, no advance guarantees. It is only love, pure, unrestrained and unlimited love" (*Can You Drink the Cup?*).

That intimacy gave Jesus the strength to drink his cup. That same intimacy Jesus wants to give to us so that we can drink ours. That intimacy has a name, a Divine Name. It is called the Holy Spirit. Living a spiritual life is living a life in which the Holy Spirit will guide us and give us the strength and courage to keep saying yes to the great questions, "Can you drink the cup? Do you love me?"

Today Jesus is telling us not to carry the cross like the Cyrenian, through fear and compulsion. Follow the Master up close, do not fear the chalice, do not fear the cross. Fear only not loving enough, that is the only real tragedy. The only real failure in the priesthood of Jesus Christ is not loving enough.

At the first Eucharist the Lord washes the feet of his disciples to give us an example, to teach us to be servants. He gives us a new commandment to love one another as he loves us. His total and sacrificial love must be the measuring stick for the love and unity, the communion, that bind us together. Then he gives us the *sacramentum caritatis*, the sacrament of love, where, as his disciples, we will find the nourishment to love as he commands us. We are the vessels of clay that carry these treasures for God's people.

Let us strive to live as his disciples, servants of the Suffering Servant, who conform our lives to his cross. Let us never forget Jesus's words, "The Son of Man came not to be served but to serve, and to give his life a ransom for many" (Matt 20:28). In giving your life you are part of the ransom.

8

REASONS BERGOGLIO BECAME A JESUIT

Each one of us priests was helped in discovering his priestly vocation because of the witness, the friendship, the advice that each of us experienced in a priest whom we knew and whose ministry touched our lives. Now it is our turn to cultivate vocations for the future. If we truly love our people, we will want them to have the blessings of the Catholic priesthood.

The Prophet Isaiah says, "You shall be called priests of the LORD,...you shall enjoy the wealth of the nations, and in their riches you shall glory" (61:6). Your ministry will produce other ministers, other priests who will serve the next generation of Catholics. Their vocations will inspire the next generation.

The way that we express our thanks for our faith and our priestly vocation is to pass these gifts on. Pope Benedict XVI said that faith is spread not by proselytizing but by attraction. I believe that is true of our vocations as well. We felt a love for the priesthood because we saw the vocation embodied in a pastor, a curate, a teacher, a missionary. As young men we were not attracted because of great retirement benefits or insurance policies that provided hair transplants, cosmetic surgery, and new dentures. No, we were attracted by the idealism and generosity of men who were good shepherds, who loved Christ and loved the people they served.

A few years ago, I was amused by the stark contrast between two vocation advertisements for the Jesuits: one in English and one in Spanish. The English one appeared on the back of *America* magazine. There was a photo of a Tom Brady clone in Brooks Brothers threads, nice jacket, and tie in a perfectly appointed state-of-the-art classroom. If you were interested, you could contact the Vocation Director at the number provided. The other advertisement was in a secular publication *El Nuevo Día*; it also depicted a Jesuit, but not in an ivory tower academic setting. It showed a young Jesuit lashed to a cross, upside down, being hurled over the Iguazú Water Falls on the border between Brazil and Paraguay. The ad featured in bold letters, "*Quieres ser Jesuita*?" The picture came from the film *The Mission*. I found it much more beguiling than the *America* ad. I recall that when I entered the seminary, I was a nerdy kid, but I wanted to become a spiritual Rambo in the jungles of Papua New Guinea. Idealism and sacrifice are attractive to young men.

Early on in the pontificate of Pope Francis, the Jesuit magazines published an interview with the Holy Father. In that interview Father Antonio Spadaro, SJ, asked Pope Francis why he became a Jesuit. The Holy Father shared with him that he was attracted to the Jesuits by three things: their missionary spirit, community, and discipline. These are not necessarily exclusively Ignatian traits, although the young Jorge Bergoglio saw them incarnate in the Jesuits of his native Buenos Aires. It is interesting to reflect on these three characteristics in our own lives.

MISSIONARY SPIRIT

Pope Francis was attracted by the missionary spirit and joined the Society of Jesus with the dream of being a missionary in Japan like St. Francis Xavier and Father Pedro Arrupe. His health was not good enough, so he remained in Argentina and discovered the need for mission there.

In *Evangelii Gaudium* Pope Francis writes, "I dream of a 'missionary option,' that is, a missionary impulse capable of transforming everything so that the Church's customs, ways of doing things, times and schedules, language and structures can be suitably channeled for the evangelization of today's world rather than for her self-preservation" (no. 27).

The Holy Father goes on to speak of "pastoral conversion." He says, "The renewal of structures demanded by pastoral conversion can only be understood in this light: as part of an effort to make them more mission-oriented, to make ordinary pastoral activity on every level more inclusive and open, to inspire in pastoral workers a constant desire to go forth and in this way to elicit a positive response from all those whom Jesus summons to friendship with himself" (no. 27).

In the Archdiocese of Boston, the program Disciples in Mission and the emphasis on evangelization is our own dream of a missionary option. We all realize that business as usual is not going to do it. We must be a missionary Church right where we are.

The Holy Father states that "the parish is not an outdated institution, precisely because it possesses great flexibility, it can assume quite different contours depending on the openness and missionary creativity of the pastor and the community." He warns against allowing the parish to become "a useless structure out of touch with people or a self-absorbed group made up of a chosen few" (no. 28). He calls on us to review and renew our parishes to bring them near to people, to make them environments of living communion and participation, and to make them completely mission-oriented.

The Holy Father urges us to say "no to pessimism." One of the more serious temptations that stifles boldness and zeal is a defeatism that turns us into querulous and disillusioned pessimists and "sourpusses" (no. 85). The Holy Father reminds us that nobody can go off to battle unless he is fully convinced of victory beforehand. If we start without confidence, we have already lost half the battle and we bury our talents. In the midst of the pastoral problems we face, our faith is challenged to discern how wine can come from water and how wheat can grow in the midst of weeds.

I am convinced that if we embrace this missionary option, our parishes will see more people responding to a priestly vocation as well as a life of Christian marriage. A missionary option will produce missionary disciples.

COMMUNITY

The second quality that the Pope mentions is community. The Holy Father is not referring to some epicurean group of similar individuals who come together for comradery and convenience. The community we need is one of brothers who come together around Christ and who share his vision, a community that is for the mission of Christ.

I never tire of encouraging our priests to join or form priestly support groups where men can come together to pray, to reflect on their own vocations, and to share each other's lives as they work together to bring Christ to his flock. The Holy Father in *Evangelii Gaudium* reminds us that "the Christian ideal will always be a summons to overcome suspicion, habitual mistrust, fear of losing our privacy, all the defensive attitudes the world imposes on us" (no. 88).

The gospel tells us constantly to run the risk of a face-to-face encounter with others, with their physical presence that challenges us, with their pain and their pleas, with their joy that infects us in our close and continuous interaction. True faith in the incarnate Son of God is inseparable from self-giving, from membership in the community, from service, from reconciliation with others.

In 2014, Boston auxiliary bishop, Robert Hennessey, invited Father Ron Knott to give the year's clergy retreat (the acupuncture Reiki instructor was not available). Father Knott is always talking about an intentional presbyterate with a corporate sense of priestly identity and mission. He is always reminding us that we are not private practitioners.

In the Ordination Rite every priest present joins the bishop in imposing hands on the ordinand and then gathers around the bishop as he prays the consecratory prayer; by doing so we participate in welcoming and celebrating the arrival of a new member into our "intimate sacramental brotherhood."

The Lord is calling us to be a family gathering, not a house divided. We are diverse in our outlooks, ethnic background, age, experience, spirituality, but we are all priests of the same presbyterate, sharing in the responsibility not only of our individual parish but also of the entire archdiocese.

In the chapter on "Temptation faced by Pastoral Workers," the Holy Father pleads with us to say "no to warring among ourselves" (nos. 98–101). We need to give the witness of authentically fraternal and reconciled communities that will help people feel attracted to the Church. In the early Church, the pagans marveled at the unity and fraternity. "See how much they love one another" was their mantra.

The Holy Father says, "It always pains me greatly to discover how some Christian communities, and even consecrated persons, can tolerate different forms of enmity, division, calumny, defamation, vendetta, jealousy and the desire to impose certain ideas at all costs, even to persecutions which appear as veritable witch hunts" (no. 100).

Our challenge is to bear witness to a constantly new way of living together in fidelity to the gospel. It is a fraternal love capable of seeing the grandeur of our neighbor, of finding God in every human being, of tolerating the nuisances of life in common by clinging to the love of God, of opening the heart to divine love and seeking the happiness of others just as their heavenly Father does.

DISCIPLINE

The third quality that attracted the young Jorge Bergoglio to his vocation was the discipline he saw in the lives of the Jesuit priests in Buenos Aires. He especially admired their use of time.

Discipline is not easy. In some ways it gets harder as you grow older, but it is no less important. Certainly, one of the greatest disciplines, as the young Bergoglio wisely perceived, is our use of time.

I never tire of urging my priests to develop a rule of life that will help ensure a certain discipline in one's life, and to guarantee the time needed to cultivate a real friendship with the Lord in prayer. Sometimes we deceive ourselves into believing that financial resources, pastoral techniques, professional trainings, and great organization are the keys to success.

True success really depends on our own faith life and vocation as priest and friend of Jesus Christ. As the Holy Father says, "The best incentive for sharing the Gospel comes from contemplating it with love, lingering over its pages and reading it with the heart. If we approach it in this way, its beauty will amaze and constantly excite us. But if this is to come about, we need to recover a contemplative spirit that can help us to realize, ever anew, that we have been entrusted with a treasure that makes us more human and helps us to lead a new life. There is nothing more precious that we can give others" (no. 264). Prayer, spiritual reading, meditation must be part of our daily routine.

There are moments in our ministry that are difficult; I call them the "Simon of Cyrene moments." As I touched on in the previous chapter, Simon was walking down the street minding his own business when those Romans snatched him and forced him to help Jesus carry the cross. I am sure that he was angry, upset, embarrassed, and frustrated. Being part of a public execution is not exactly on everyone's bucket list. I am sure that he must have felt that it was the worst day of his life.

The New Testament tells us very little about Simon of Cyrene. We only know that he was African, and that he had two sons, Alexander and Rufus. Some scholars have identified these two sons with men who were later leaders in the Christian community. I like to think that Simon's experience of carrying the cross is what led to his conversion and eventually to the conversion of his entire family. Poor Simon was minding his own business when those bullying Roman soldiers picked him out of the crowd, possibly because of the color of his skin, and made him part of a humiliating spectacle of the crucifixion. What began as the worst day of his life was really the best day, something he came to realize much later.

We all have Simon of Cyrene moments in our ministry. Those are the difficult things that we would rather not do, but we have no escape. We all have moments when we could say, "I'd rather be having a root canal." Yes, we all have Simon of Cyrene moments. We do it, but we would rather not. Human respect, fear of criticism, a despotic bishop, Irish guilt. Powerful motivators. All of us have things we have to do, that we dread, but you know what? Those worst days of our life are probably the most important things that we can do as a priest. In my own ministry, I know this to be the case.

During Lent I love to pray the Stations, and I often linger on the contrast between the Fifth and the Sixth Stations. In the Fifth Station the Cyrenian is being forced to carry the cross. Inside he is whining and feeling sorry for himself and can't wait for this to end.

In the Sixth Station, Veronica overcomes all human expectations and regard for her personal safety or her reputation. She forces her way through the crowd that is always pushing us away from Christ. She only wants to provide the slightest service to comfort Christ, to be present to him and wipe his bloodied face. It is courage, generosity that puts the needs of others first. This legendary woman represents all those disciples who boldly overcome the fear of the cross in order to be a sign of God's mercy to those who are suffering and those who seem to be beyond help.

How do we move from being the character in the Fifth Station who has to be forced to do good, to becoming like the one in the Sixth Station who does the right thing, boldly and enthusiastically?

That is the discipline that the young Jorge Bergoglio saw in the priests and religious he admired and who inspired him in his vocation. It is the kind of discipline that makes time and space for God in our daily routine.

It is the discipline that allows us to overcome our fear of the cross. Fear of the cross is what causes us to be mediocre. Love casts out that fear and allows us to face Calvary. It is not easy. Of the first priests, only the youngest one stood by the cross. He was terrified but his love allowed him to overcome all fear and to stand at the foot of the cross.

This is the discipline we need in our ministry, especially in our service of the sick and the poor. The Holy Father challenges us to see Lazarus suffering, covered with sores, on our doorstep. The Holy Father says our preferential love for the poor must translate into pastoral care for the poor and the suffering. We must look for ways to bring the word of God and the sacraments to them. As the Holy Father states so clearly, "None of us can think we are exempt from concern for the poor and for social justice" (no. 201).

It requires great discipline to be able to respond to the demands on our time and the many challenges of ministry. Our task is to allow the world to glimpse the love and mercy of the Good Shepherd who is always seeking the lost sheep, not to condemn but to console. Like the Greeks in the gospel who wanted to see Jesus, our people want to glimpse Jesus in us, in our kindness, mercy, and loving response to their pain and suffering. We often find ourselves where Simon of Cyrene was. Only a person with discipline in their life will have the freedom to respond.

It is the discipline that we will attain only by having that personal rule of life that provides for prayer, spiritual reading, confession, and priestly fraternity.

The joy of the gospel that can make our ministry an expression of joy requires apostolic zeal, priestly fraternity, and discipline. At the same time these are qualities that will inspire young men to respond to the call of a vocation without having to throw our vocations director over Niagara Falls on a cross.

I never use props for my homilies. Kevin O'Leary in his children's Mass uses some with great skill. I was once at Holy Name Church for the very moving ceremony and funeral Mass for a fireman who died in a tragic fire. I featured the beautiful mosaic over the altar in my blog. It is a replica of the mosaic in the historic church of San Clemente in Rome. Subsequently, Pastoral Associate Fran Hauck sent me a copy of the cross as depicted in the Mosaic. It is very unusual, for the cross appears in the apse of San Clemente as the tree of life; at the foot of the cross a deer is drinking, and nearby there is a dead snake, but on the cross are a series of birds.

I was going to consult with Boston Auxiliary Bishop John Boles, an amateur ornithologist, but I decided to consult with the ancient and renowned theological authority of Wikipedia and discovered that the doves on the San Clemente Cross represent the twelve apostles, perched on the cross, poised to fly to the ends of the earth to announce Christ's victory.

I thought about that. It occurred to me that on Good Friday there were not twelve doves on the cross. There was only one young priest nervously accompanying our Blessed Lady. The cross reminds us that the very apostles who fled from the cross into the witness protection program at the Cenacle safe house, later returned to embrace the cross after Pentecost. Christ gave them another chance to overcome their fear of the cross. The irony is that all the apostles died as martyrs except the one who actually went to Calvary.

If we do not have missionary zeal in our ministry, if we are not striving to form a communion with our fellow priests in an intentional presbyterate, if we do not have discipline in our lives especially in our use of time, a precious commodity, we must ask ourselves if we are fleeing from the cross.

Nearly sixteen years ago I entered the doors of Holy Cross Cathedral for the installation ceremony. Outside there was a sea of demonstrators and media. The ceremony began with a powerful symbol: I was presented with a cross to kiss. I confess it was a Simon of Cyrene moment.

But it was also an opportunity to rediscover my identity as a bishop and to be reminded of what St. Paul wrote to Timothy, "For this reason I remind you to rekindle the gift of God that is within you through the laying on of my hands; for God did not give us a spirit of cowardice, but rather a spirit of power and of love and of self-discipline. Do not be ashamed, then, of the testimony about our Lord or of me his prisoner, but join with me in suffering for the gospel, relying on the power of God" (2 Tim 1:6–8).

During a retreat, we have another chance to fly to the cross and be renewed together with our brother priests. Our ordination promises are the vows of love and fidelity that we made to Christ and to our people. After stirring the gifts into flame, like the apostles may we fly back to our people to announce Christ's victory and the joy of the gospel.

9

A JESUIT-FRANCISCAN POPE

I have always liked the story about the Jesuit and the Franciscan who are walking down the street one day when suddenly they are accosted by a young man who says to them, "Fathers, can you tell me what novena I should make to acquire a BMW?" The Franciscan asked, "What is a BMW?" And the Jesuit asked, "What's a novena?"

We have a pope who defies these categories and seems to have melded the Jesuit and the Franciscan into one. But I believe that Pope Francis is the quintessential Ignatian Jesuit.

My observations are not due to the benefits of a Jesuit education, of which I have no personal experience, but I describe my situation as being like those nonsmokers who consider themselves a victim of secondhand smoke. My dad, my uncle, and my older brother were all formed in the faith by faith-filled sons of St. Ignatius, and all of them have lived lives that reflect love for Christ and the Church and fidelity in their vocations as husbands, fathers, and Catholic laymen with a sense of the Church's social gospel as well as the spirituality of the *Exercises*.

In his talk to major superiors of religious, Pope Francis expressed his admiration for Father Segundo Llorente, SJ, who was a missionary in Alaska for forty years, an example of going to the periphery. In 1960, Father Segundo was elected to the Alaska State Legislature as a write-in candidate. His memoir is called *Forty Years in the Arctic Circle*.

For forty years, I was a very close collaborator of his brother, Padre Amando Llorente, who was also a great Jesuit who transformed lives with his ministry as head of the Agrupación Católica and an outstanding preacher and director of souls. One of Father Llorente's most famous students was Fidel Castro. That too is going to the periphery.

Miguel de Unamuno wrote a biography of Don Quixote—the protagonist of Cervantes's masterpiece, which is probably the most influential novel ever written (before *The Da Vinci Code* by Dan Brown, of course). Unamuno began his biography with an ingenious comparison of Don Quixote and St. Ignatius of Loyola, drawing from Cervantes's description of the man of La Mancha and Rivadeneira's biography of the founder of the Jesuits.

Both individuals were greatly influenced by their voracious reading. Unamuno describes how Ignatius set out for Monserrat to deposit his arms at the feet of the Virgin. On the road to Monserrat, he encountered a Moor who insulted the Blessed Mother. Ignatius tried to convince him, without success, and the Moor rode away very conceited and arrogant.

The young Ignatius had second thoughts and wondered if he should have punished the man or at least injured him. He decided to let God decide by dropping the reins of his steed to see if the animal would pursue the recalcitrant Moor or continue following the road to the sanctuary of Monserrat. The beast trotted off to Monserrat and the Jesuit Order was founded because of a decision made by a humble donkey, which could in a certain sense be credited with the founding of the Society of Jesus.

The early biographers recount how St. Ignatius was wounded in the battle of Pamplona, and how he spent much of his convalescence reading. Because there were no books of chivalry like Quixote and Ignatius loved to read, they gave the patient Ludwig of Saxons's *Life of Christ* and a florilegium of the lives of the saints. After devouring the books, Ignatius commented, "I want to be a saint like St. Francis."

We have a pope who has embraced the vocation of being a follower of Ignatius, "who want[ed] to be a saint like St. Francis."

Our pope is thoroughly Jesuit, thoroughly Ignatian, right down to the fascination with St. Francis. In his interview in *Civiltà Çattolica,* Father Antonio Spadaro, SJ, asked Pope Francis why he became a Jesuit. The pope said three things about the Jesuits that attracted him were the missionary spirit, community, and discipline. He especially admired the way the Jesuits manage their time.

It is obvious that Pope Francis exhibits these characteristics in spades. He is truly living his Jesuit vocation with an intense missionary zeal, a love for community, a community for mission, and the disciplined life that does not waste anything, especially time.

Shortly before his ordination, the thirty-two-year-old Bergoglio wrote a short "credo." He has kept that piece of paper as a reminder of his core convictions. It is a clear indication of the habit of self-reflection so deeply ingrained by his Jesuit formation.

First, he recognizes that he is flawed, recognizing his own selfishness, his "egotism in which I take refuge." But the young Bergoglio also professes his conviction that God has given him gifts to be used in the service of God's people.

He speaks of his own history and says that on a spring day in September (Southern Hemisphere! Just one indication of a new perspective, a new vantage point in the Church), "the loving face of God crossed my path and invited me to follow Him." The Holy Father is always harkening back to the day of his own spiritual awakening and conversion on the Feast of St. Matthew, which found him breaking away from his friends to go to church to receive the sacrament of confession. It was there that he first felt called. Later, he shared that his favorite painting in Rome is Caravaggio's *Calling of Matthew*, where Jesus is pointing at the tax collector. Bergoglio said that when he looks at that painting, he feels that Jesus is pointing at him. It is not surprising that Father Bergoglio, when appointed bishop, chose the phrase *miserando atque eligendo* from the homily of the Venerable Bede on the Feast of St. Matthew, the publican converted and called to be an apostle.

The experience as a seventeen-year-old was in his words "the astonishment of an encounter…of encountering someone who was waiting for you….God is the one who seeks us first." The Holy Father views morality in the context of an encounter with Christ that is "triggered by mercy": "the privileged locus of the encounter is the caress of the mercy of Jesus Christ on our sins, and thus a new morality—a correspondence to mercy is born." He views this morality as a "revolution"; it is not a titanic effort of the will, but simply a response to a surprising, unforeseeable, and "unjust mercy." Morality is not a "never falling down," but "an always getting up again."

Pope Francis embraces the introspection that is so central to Jesuit spirituality. The practice of the *examen*, undertaken individually wherever and whenever the circumstances permitted, was Ignatius's plan to keep the Jesuits recollected in God—focused, despite their active lifestyles.

As novice master, Father Jorge insisted on fidelity to the practice of *examen*, realizing that Ignatius's strict program of formation was to prepare men for years of discipline once all the props of the formation program were taken away.

There are many indications that Pope Francis is very comfortable in his own skin and does not feel constrained by former practices of pontificates in the past. But one of the most striking examples of this clarity of vision and confidence is his decision to go to the juvenile detention center Casal del Marmo to wash the feet of a group of prisoners.

On Holy Thursday, Jesus washed the feet of the Twelve. They were shocked and unhinged by the experience. St. Peter rebelled at the thought but capitulated when Jesus insisted. For most of us, it has become a rather stylized liturgical gesture that is but a reflection of what the original foot washing entailed. Pope Francis replicated the surprise, the shock of the apostles, as he dismayed those who preferred the stylized liturgy in a basilica.

This was not an innovation for Pope Francis; as archbishop of Buenos Aires, he had been doing this each Holy Week. The Holy Father was jostling our imagination because we have grown so complacent that we can no longer see beyond the familiar custom to glimpse the challenging truth. With a simple gesture, the pope was challenging core assumptions about power, authority, and leadership. As he told the prisoners, this is a symbol, it is a sign. "Washing your feet," he said, "means I am at your service."

On July 27, 2013, in his address to the Brazilian bishops at World Youth Day, Pope Francis said, "Unless we train ministers capable of warming peoples' hearts, of walking with them in the night, of dialoguing with their hopes and disappointments, of mending their brokenness, what joy can we have for our present and future journey?"

One of Father Jorge's former novices recounts how Father Bergoglio always insisted that the seminarians should go on the weekends to the poorest *barrios* to give catechism classes to the children. He used to tell them that if someone could make the catechism simple enough for children to understand, that was a wise person. When the seminarians returned from the poor neighborhoods, Father Bergoglio would always check to see if they had dusty shoes. If a seminarian did not have dusty shoes, that man had some explaining to do.

This same desire to teach the young Jesuits to stay engaged with the people, to be close to the little people, is what Jesus did when he was training the apostles. Jesus took them to the temple to observe the widow putting her last penny into the collection. The Lord does not refund her money, applaud her, nor give her a compliment. She is unaware that she is being observed as Jesus uses her as part of his lesson plan to his seminarian apostles. He helps them to see the poor widow through his eyes. Jesus wants his priests to see the faith and the devotion of the *anawim*, the poor who are rich in faith.

In *Evangelii Gaudium*, Pope Francis reminds us that God's heart has a special place for the poor, so much so that he himself "became poor." The entire history of our redemption is marked by the presence of the poor. In his inaugural address at the synagogue in Nazareth, Jesus uses the prophecy of Isaiah to describe his own messianic mission: "The Spirit of the Lord is upon me because he has anointed me to preach good news to the poor." Jesus assured those burdened by sorrow and crushed by poverty that God has a special place for them in his heart: blessed are the poor, yours is the kingdom of heaven.

Pope Francis is most eloquent in his advocacy on behalf of the poor and our obligation to help them by programs of promotion and assistance, as well as by working to resolve the structural causes of poverty. However, one of Pope Francis's most impassioned pleas on behalf of the poor concerns their pastoral care. Again, in *Evangelii Gaudium*, the Holy Father writes,

> I want to say with regret that the worst discrimination which the poor suffer is the lack of spiritual care. The great majority of the poor have a special openness to the faith; they need God and we must not fail to offer them His friendship, His blessing, His Word, the celebration of the sacraments and a journey of growth and maturity in the faith. Our preferential option for the poor must mainly translate into a privileged and preferential religious care. (no. 200)

Reading this passage reminds me of something that happened years ago when I was working at the Centro Católico. There had been a terrible earthquake in Guatemala and thousands of people perished. A former priest who was working at a secular relief organization came to seek my help in contacting some remote indigenous people in Guatemala. His agency wanted to fund a project for the poorest people.

I arranged for a friend to take this individual to a remote mountain village where he made known his agency's offer to this people. He told them to choose any one project: a school, a clinic, or a well. The elders of the tribe asked for time to discuss the proposal with the members of the tribe. After their deliberations, the chief returned and said to the former priest, "Sir, what we need more than anything else is new doors for our Church."

Needless to say, my friend was shocked and embarrassed. I am not sure how he negotiated that with his agency.

The interesting thing is that the indigenous people, despite all their physical needs, felt that their relationship with God was their most pressing need. Pope Francis would have understood that immediately.

The young Jorge Bergoglio joined the Jesuits partly out of a desire to be a missionary in Japan. It is hard to read Pope Francis's challenge to go to the peripheries without recalling the letter of Francis Xavier to St. Ignatius that appears in the breviary for the feast of the great Jesuit missionary:

> Many, many people are not becoming Christians for one reason only: There is nobody to make them Christians. Again and again, I have thought of going around to the Universities of Europe, especially Paris, and everywhere crying out like a madman, riveting the attention of those with more learning than charity: "What a tragedy: How many souls are being shut out of heaven and falling into hell, thanks to you!" I wish they would work as hard at this as they do at their books and so settle their account with God for the learning and talents entrusted to them.

Pope Francis never got to be a missionary to Japan but he never ceased to admire those Jesuit missionaries and others who formed the faith of the laity so well that those Christian communities in Japan went without priests for over 250 years. In 1865, two years after Mathew Perry opened Japan to foreigners, Father Bernard Petitjean of the Missions étrangères de Paris opened a Church for foreign nationals but was immediately visited by throngs of underground Catholics who had practiced their faith clandestinely. The French priest found them all baptized, catechized, and legitimately married in the Church, and all their dead had received a Christian burial.

As Pope Francis observes, "Faith was kept intact by the gifts of grace that gladdened the lives of the laity, who only received baptism but then continued to live their apostolic mission."

Pope Francis, like Pope Benedict, has said that Catholicism is not a "catalogue of prohibitions." He urges us to be positive, to emphasize the things that unite us, not the negative, the things that divide us. "You must prioritize the connection between people, the path we walk together. After that, addressing the differences becomes easier."

The Holy Father says that "every form of catechesis would do well to attend to the 'way of beauty' (*via pulchritudinis*)," showing that to follow Christ "is not only something right and true but also something beautiful, capable of filling life with new splendor and profound joy, even in the midst of difficulties" (*EG* 167).

> As for the moral component of catechesis, which promotes growth in fidelity to the Gospel way of life, it is helpful to stress again and again the attractiveness and the ideal of a life of wisdom, self-fulfillment and enrichment. In the light of that positive message, our rejection of the evils which endanger that life can be better understood. Rather than experts in dire predictions, dour judges bent on rooting out every threat and deviation, we should appear as joyful messengers of challenging proposals, guardians of the goodness and beauty which shine forth in a life of fidelity to the Gospel. (*EG* 168)

The faith of the Church corresponds to a vision of reality that gives value to every human being, insisting on our responsibility to love and serve one another, especially the most vulnerable among us. Pope Francis has been asking us to embrace this vision of reality. The word Pope Francis uses repeatedly is *tenerezza*, "tenderness." At the Feast of St. Joseph, during the Mass at the beginning of his pontificate, the pope told us of the need to protect people, to care lovingly for each other, particularly the children, the elderly, and the needy, who often are the last who come to mind. The pope said, "We should not be afraid of kindness or tenderness," and he gave us as an example the heart of St. Joseph. In St. Joseph, tenderness is not the virtue of the weak, but the sign of strength of mind, the capacity to take care and have compassion, a genuine openness to others, to love.

Some people think that the Holy Father should talk more about abortion. I have to say that he speaks of love and mercy to give everyone the context of the Church's teachings on abortion. We are against abortion, not because we are mean or old-fashioned, but because we love people. And that is what we need to show the world.

I recently read the testimony of a volunteer in Africa who told of his experience in a refugee camp at the time of food distribution. The situation was chaotic, even frightening. He could see that the food was running out and the starving people were desperate. The last person at the end of the line was a nine-year-old girl. When it was her turn, there was only one banana left. They handed it to her. She peeled the banana, gave one half to the younger brother and the other half to the younger sister. Then she licked the banana peel. The volunteer confessed that at that moment he began to believe in God.

We must be better people; we have to love everyone, even those who advocate abortion. Only our love can help them discover that the life of an unborn child is sacred. Our love and mercy will be able to open hearts hardened by the individualism of our time.

In the United States, we are an immigrant church. It is very significant that the first visit of the Holy Father was to Lampedusa to underline his concern about the fate of migrants.

Laying a wreath on this sea where thousands of North African refugees died crammed into authentic coffin boats, the pope spoke of the globalization of indifference, indifference to the suffering of others, to the future of the unborn, to the future of the elderly, the mentally and physically handicapped, and migrants.

We will have to overcome this indifference in our own lives to show others that the teachings of the Church have to do with loving and caring for all. In his address to the Brazilian bishops, Pope Francis said, "We need a Church capable of rediscovering the maternal womb of mercy. Without mercy, we have little chance today to enter into a world of 'wounded,' who need understanding, forgiveness, love." The Holy Father says that mercy without truth would be consolation without honesty and is nothing but empty talk. The merciless truth, however, is cold; it alienates and hurts. The truth is not a wet rag to be thrown in one's face but a warm cloak with which to cuddle up to be protected and get strong.

Our efforts to heal society's wounds will depend on our ability to love and to be true to our mission. The Holy Father has shown us very clearly that our battle is not just a political struggle nor a legal issue, but that we need to evangelize and humanize culture. Only then will the world be a safe place for the unborn, the elderly, and those who are unproductive. The gospel of life is a gospel of mercy. We can only be heard in today's world if people recognize the authenticity of our lives and our commitment to building a civilization of love. We are called to live our lives as a service to others and to live it in a way that bears witness to the presence of God's love and mercy among us.

I have always enjoyed the story of the man who was seriously ill and went to the doctor for several tests. At one point the doctor asked to speak with his wife. He explained to her that her husband's situation was very difficult and that he was in danger of life. There was only one chance he could get better: if she treated him very well. The woman asked, "What does that mean?" The doctor replied that she should cook only the meals he liked best, allow him to go fishing with his friends, give him the television remote control, not ask him to mow the lawn or take out the trash, and keep the children and mother-in-law at a distance. The doctor insisted, "If you do all these things, there is a strong chance that your husband will survive." In the car on the way home, the frightened husband asked his wife, "What did the doctor tell you?" She replied, "Honey, the doctor said you're going to die."

Our ministry and service in the Church is like this story: if we don't do that extra—even beyond reasonable—if we don't go beyond the request, if we don't share the coat beside the tunic, if we don't present the other face, then the patient will die.

As St. Augustine said, "Without God we can do nothing; without us, God will do nothing."

The Holy Father Pope Francis says that the face of God is mercy and so the face of the Church must be mercy. It is an invitation to live and witness the joy of the gospel. Thank God we have this Jesuit-Franciscan pope who, with gestures and words, teaches us to do so.

Conference at Catholic University of Portugal,
Lisbon, June 28, 2016

PART II

To the Rhythm of Liturgy and Mission

10

PRAYING WITHOUT DISTRACTIONS

It is very fitting that the Scriptures are calling us at the beginning of Lent to reflect on prayer, which is so central to our spiritual life. Many years ago, I heard a story about two men who were involved in a conversation about prayer. One of them was bragging about how much he liked to pray and how easy it was for him. His companion lamented that he had great difficulty in prayer and was plagued by distractions. The first man claimed that he never had any distractions. His friend found that too difficult to accept and proposed a wager. He said, "I'll bet you can't say the Our Father, without a distraction." To which his friend said, "That is so simple, I accept your bet." But what will you give me if I win? The man replied, "If you can say the Our Father, without one distraction, I will give you my horse." His friend knelt down and very piously began to pray: "Our Father, who art in heaven, hallowed be thy name....Do I get the saddle too?"

Prayer is not easy. In the Gospel, we see Jesus as a great teacher of prayer. In Matthew's Gospel, we have Jesus's teachings about prayer directed to those Christians coming out of a Jewish background. They were people with a long tradition of prayer and liturgy. Their greatest difficulty was to avoid falling into a formalism, so Jesus invites the people to go to a room and pray to the Father in secret rather than being like the Pharisees praying in public in order to be praised. The challenge is to pray with ardor, and from the heart. The words are not that important. Rather, it is the faith—the trust in the other in our heart—that makes our prayers real. So, in today's Gospel, Jesus tells his followers not to babble on like the pagans.

In Luke's Gospel, Jesus is teaching those who have come to the faith from paganism, like St. Luke, himself. They do not enjoy that same tradition of spirituality, discipline, and fidelity to prayer. Hence, in Luke's Gospel, Jesus emphasizes the importance of perseverance in prayer, to pray always, without giving up, like the widow badgering the unjust judge.

In today's Gospel, Jesus is giving us the Our Father, the model for all Christian prayer. In the history of the Church this precious prayer was part of the *disciplina arcani*. It was taught to neophytes only after they had begun their process of initiation into the faith. The prayer was considered very precious and such a privilege because through this prayer Jesus is inviting us to join with his prayer, to make his words and sentiments our own. The formula of introduction for the prayer in the liturgy contains the words *audemus dicere*, "we dare to say." It requires boldness to call God our Father and to associate ourselves with Christ in the intimate moment of communication with the Father.

The great British historian Toynbee has said that the history of civilization is a history of the various concepts of God that have formed different religions and civilizations. The mythology of the Greeks and the Romans portrays a multiplicity of gods whose vices and defects are made in imitation and likeness to humanity. The god of the Enlightenment was the great clockmaker who wound up the clock, cast it into space, and then turned his back and walked away. For the Aztecs, their gods were bloodthirsty beings demanding human sacrifices in order to coax them to advance from one season to another.

When Jesus teaches us to pray, he begins by teaching us the concept of God that must shape everything in our spiritual life. God is the Father. In fact, when we use this word to describe God, we mean that he is more father than any human father could ever be. Hence, Jesus says, "Call no man father because no human father can be as much a father as God who is our Creator, our Sanctifier and Redeemer, who loves us more than anyone else, who is always there to care for us, to forgive us, to reward and punish us, but most of all to love us."

So, in prayer we are speaking not with some impersonal distant deity but with our Father who has brought us into existence because of love, and his love for us never fails. He is our Father, not just my Father, because we are all his children, his creatures. We are brothers and sisters. Because God is so good and so loving, our first impulse must be to praise him, and to declare that his name is holy.

Among the petitions of the Our Father, the ones that are most central are *Thy kingdom come, Thy will be done*. Often when we pray, what we really mean is, my kingdom come, my will be done. However, Jesus wants us to be so aware of our Father's loving providence that we can say with freedom and trust, *Thy will be done*. This is the heart of all Christian prayer, and indeed, in the New Testament the three greatest prayers all express this same attitude of trust and of actively embracing God's will in our life: Mary's *fiat*; Jesus's prayer at Gethsemane; and the Our Father.

The Gospel begins with Mary's *fiat*: "Be it done unto me according to thy word." God is knocking on the door of humanity, and Mary opens that door in our name. Mother Teresa used to always say, "Give God permission." That's what Mary does at the annunciation. In the agony in the Garden, the prayer that Jesus repeats over and over again is "Not my will, but thine be done." And these are the very sentiments that Jesus is teaching us in the Lord's Prayer: "Thy kingdom come, thy will be done." Because God is all loving, and all-powerful, and all good, what he wills and desires is far better than anything we could contrive.

Jesus teaches us to trust in God's love, in the Father's love. And so, we ask for his will to be done in our lives and we ask for today's bread, not tomorrow's, because we trust that tomorrow God will give to us when we ask. When Moses told the Israelites to gather the manna, he said only take as much as you need for today. Those who disobeyed because of their lack of trust and their selfishness discovered that the extra manna rotted.

This prayer also contains a very dangerous petition where we ask God to forgive our sins in the same way that we forgive others. Now, for the Irish, this is very difficult. It is said that Irish Alzheimer's is when you forget everything except the grudges. Forgiveness does not come easy. We must see it as part of the way that we embrace the will of the Father, who demands us to be merciful, the way that he is merciful sending his sun on the good and evil, and his rain on the just and the unjust.

During this holy season of Lent, let us ask our blessed Savior for the grace of prayer. And let us dare to pray the Our Father, the way that Blessed Charles de Foucauld did at Nazareth, where his reflections on the Lord's Prayer are contained in his prayer of abandonment:

Father, I abandon myself into your hands;
do with me what you will.
Whatever you may do,
I thank you:
I am ready for all,
I accept all.
Let only your will be done in me,
and in all your creatures.
I wish no more than this, O Lord.
Into your hands I commend my soul:
I offer it to you with all the love of my heart.
For I love you, Lord,
and so need to give myself,
to surrender myself into your hands
without reserve,
and with boundless trust,
for you are my Father.

11

JONAH

There is this story of a woman who went to her son's room to wake him up on Sunday morning. She bangs on the door and shouts, "Johnny, get up. It's late. It's time for Mass." Her son replies, "Do I have to?" The mother shouts back, "Yes, you have to!" The son answers, "But Mom, why do I have to get up?" To which she answers, "Johnny, because you are forty-five years old, you are a priest, and the pastor of this parish."

There are two figures that emerge each Lent that speak to me in a special way. I have already talked about one of them, Simon of Cyrene, the reluctant cross bearer. The other is Jonah, the reluctant prophet.

Jonah does not want to be the messenger of God to the people of Nineveh. He knows that people often shoot the messenger. Nor does he have any affection for the people of Nineveh. He tries to escape God's plan for him by stowing away on the ship. We know how that story ends: the crew throws him overboard, and he is devoured by a huge fish. Three days later, he is deposited on the shore and continues his mission.

This reluctant prophet receives attention from Jesus in the Gospels. In Matthew, Jesus talks about the sign of Jonah, his three-day sojourn in the belly of a whale, an obvious sign of the resurrection. In today's Gospel from Luke, Jesus speaks of Jonah as a sign to the people of Nineveh. The sign is his preaching, God's message that he carried to the people of Nineveh. That sign is so convincing that the people of Nineveh are converted and do penance for their sins.

It is almost comical to see Jonah's petulant reaction: Jonah feels that God forgiving the people of Nineveh makes the messenger look foolish.

Although we bishops are at times like the reluctant Simon carrying the cross because we are coerced, and like the reluctant Jonah, preaching the gospel because we have to, Lent should be a time for us truly to embrace our mission and overcome our reluctance—our lack of generosity, the lack of courage that makes us like Simon and Jonah.

The great city of Nineveh is all around us. The morality of the Ten Commandments has been rejected by the modern culture. The only commandment that seems to have any traction is this: thou shall not smoke. The gospel of love, service, morality, and social justice does not have the same influence over society as political correctness, consumerism, materialism, and hedonism. Preaching the gospel of repentance can seem a thankless task.

The solution is not for us to run and hide, but to look for ways that we can grow together in our vocation and mission. We must be the sign of Jonah for the Nineveh of today. The sign of Jonah is, first, the sign of the resurrection. People living in a culture of death long for the gospel of life. There are many ways that the Church announces and witnesses to the resurrection of Jesus Christ. The first and most obvious witness was that of the martyrs who, in shedding their blood, faced death and torment with the assurance that they would live forever in the resurrection.

When the bloody persecution subsided, the new sign

of Jonah was consecrated virginity and celibacy, the white martyrdom. In a world where people interpreted immortality as living on in their descendants, those early Christians who embraced celibacy, in imitation of Jesus, were saying to the world that not everyone needs to get married and have children to survive. We are all called to live forever in the resurrection of Christ.

The sign of Jonah is always visible in the radical renunciations that believers do in the name of the gospel, whether that be the evangelical counsels or a life of faithful discipleship in whatever vocation God gives to us. The sign of Jonah is also announcing the gospel in words and through deeds. Pope Francis often speaks about the need for *vicinanza*, "closeness to God's people." We must always seek new ways to be closer to our people and bring them the message of the gospel and allow them to hear the call to conversion, to community, to discipleship. We must not allow ourselves to become antagonistic or dismissive of the people of Nineveh. We must not see them as enemies, but as potential conversions—possible brothers and sisters in the family of the Church.

In my own life, I came to know and appreciate Dr. Bernard Nathanson, who was the founder of the abortion movement in the United States. He personally aborted thousands of unborn babies. But, like Saul who persecuted the Church and became the great apostle of the Gentiles, Bernard Nathanson became the voice and face of the pro-life movement. He was one of the Ninevites who experienced a profound conversion and sense of mercy.

Lent is not just a time to give up whiskey or candy or movies. For us bishops, it should be a time when we're working to overcome everything in our hearts that makes us reluctant to embrace the cross or to announce the good news of the gospel. The urgent message is that we have forty days to do it.

12

PRAYER IS HEEDED

In the Gospel, Jesus assures us that prayer is answered. In Luke's Gospel, we read about the annunciation of St. John the Baptist. Zachariah is told, "Your prayers have been answered." For years, he and his wife, Elizabeth, had prayed every day to be blessed with a child. Now as an old man, he is confronted by a vision of an angel that tells him he will be a father. He is unable to believe that is possible. Because of his lack of belief, he is struck dumb. How ironic.

Sometimes, we can be the same, praying but without the conviction that our prayers make a difference. Jesus's teaching on prayer in today's Gospel is to assure us of the efficacy of prayer: "Ask and it will be given you; seek and you shall find; knock and the door will be opened to you. For everyone who asks, receives, and the one who seeks, finds; and to the one who knocks, the door will be opened."

Jesus reminds us that, despite our own sinfulness, we are capable of giving good things to our family. Our Heavenly Father is even more generous in the good gifts that he gives to his children.

The power of prayer is demonstrated in history. A wicked ruler was preparing to eliminate all the Jews in the kingdom. Queen Esther turns to God in prayer: "God of Abraham, God of Isaac, and God of Jacob, blessed are you. Help me who am alone and have no help but you, come to help me, an orphan. Save us from the hand of our enemy."

But Esther was not an orphan. God hears her prayer and changes the course of history. Each year, the Jewish people celebrate the Feast of Purim. It is a joyful remembrance of God's intervention in history that saved the people in a moment of great danger.

An important part of our ministry as bishops is to be men of prayer. The Church has given us the responsibility of the breviary, a prayer that allows us to be in touch with the rhythms of the liturgical year, marking the great events of the history of salvation. The Liturgy of the Hours allows us to extend the Eucharistic Prayer to the whole day. We should not have the attitude of Cardinal Richelieu, who used to wait until later in the evening and then prayed all the hours together. He postponed praying the breviary until night in case he would die during the day and thus be excused from the obligation.

Faithfully praying the Liturgy of the Hours can mold our hearts and minds. When we read the Seven Last Words of Jesus, we see how the psalms that Jesus prayed each day sprung from his life as he faced death on the Cross.

The Liturgy of the Hours, even when prayed alone, are connecting us to all our fellow priests and religious and faithful, who are uniting their prayer to that of Christ as we praise our Heavenly Father and beseech his blessings and mercy upon the whole Body of Christ and the world.

A bishop named Alvaro summoned one of his priests and reprimanded him for the way the priest was praying for him during the canon of the Mass. The priest was saying, "We pray for our Pope Francis and for our bishop, your unworthy servant Alvaro."

As bishops, we are fortunate that the very formulas of the liturgy oblige our priests and people to pray for us at every Mass even when they consider us as unworthy servants.

The Gospel gives us the Golden Rule: "Do unto others whatever you would have them do to you." Another wording of the Great Command: "Love God above all and love your neighbor as yourself." As Jesus says, "This is the Law and the Prophets."

Just as the liturgy provides for our people to pray for us, the people of God count on our prayers. It is hardly possible to visit someone in the hospital without being asked to enter several rooms to bless the sick and say a prayer for those who are suffering from some illness or who have suffered an accident or an operation. A very important part of our ministry is to pray for the people entrusted to our care. We need to make sure we never cease to intercede for their needs.

One bishop once said that the three favorite lies of priests are the following: I have no money...that woman is my sister...and I will pray for you. So often, we promise people our prayers. Such a promise should never be an empty formula, a meaningless phrase! Our promise to pray is simply renewing the commitment we made on the day of our ordination as a deacon, on the day of our ordination as a priest, and on the day of our ordination as a bishop.

In fact, in the ordination to the diaconate, we were asked if we were resolved to maintain and deepen the spirit of prayer and to celebrate faithfully the Liturgy of the Hours with and for the people of God and indeed for the whole world.

As priests, we were asked to resolve to implore God's mercy upon the people entrusted to our care by observing the command to pray without ceasing.

As bishops, we are asked to pray without ceasing to almighty God for the holy people.

At every step, the Church reminds us of our duty to be men of prayer and intercessors on behalf of God's people.

13

"HOWEVER, I SAY TO YOU"

Jesus offers six vivid illustrations of the surpassing righteousness to which he calls his disciples. He sets up these examples with the phrase, "You have heard that it was said" or "It was also said," introducing either a quote from or an allusion to the Law, sometimes with the mention of how the Law was understood and applied. This is followed by the words, "But I say to you," which mark a solemn pronouncement by Jesus, bringing forth the deeper meaning of the Law and how it is to be lived out in the kingdom.

In the Greek text, the "I" in the statement, "But I say to you" is most emphatic. Jesus presents his teaching with the same authority as that by which God gave the Law to Moses. This must certainly have aroused the attention of his listeners.

The first example we have in the Gospel concerns the laws against murder. Jesus calls for an interiorization of the Law that touches one's motives, thoughts, and attitudes, but in no way lessens the Law's literal force. Jesus called his disciples to a higher standard than that of the scribes and Pharisees, and he brings out the true meaning of the Law. External conforming to the Law is not enough. The Law must be interiorized so that it penetrates one's heart and leads one to live according to God's ultimate intentions.

Jesus does not want us merely to avoid killing one another; he calls us to remove the attitudes and actions that lead to killing and, indeed, every obstacle to unconditional love. Jesus quotes the Fifth Commandment, "Thou shalt not kill," but he goes beyond the letter of the Law, calling people to avoid even the kind of anger and critical speech that seeks to wound another person, and thus destroys relationships. Whoever is angry with his brother or publicly dishonors him by calling him *Raqa*, which means "imbecile" or "idiot," will face severe punishment.

The next two illustrations underscore the importance of not letting anger persist. Jesus addresses the person who is about to offer sacrifice but remembers an unresolved problem in a personal relationship. Jesus says, "Leave your gift there at the altar, go first and be reconciled with your brother." Spoken in Galilee, this dramatic picture might suggest a Galilean leaving his animal at the altar in the temple in Jerusalem and going all the way back to his home to be reconciled with his brother before returning to complete the sacrifice. This hyperbole would accentuate the urgency to resolve any tensions in a relationship rather than let them fester.

With his next illustration, Jesus challenges his disciples to settle with your opponent quickly while on the way to court with him. If you succeed in reaching an out-of-court settlement, Jesus suggests that you avoid the risk that the divine judge will render judgment against you. In one of the translations of this Gospel, the word for "settle with your opponent" is rendered by the phrase "to make friends." Responding to your accuser with anger only increases hostility, but goodwill and a desire to be reconciled helps restore friendship. The dramatic image of being thrown into prison points to the consequence of not seeking reconciliation with one's opponent.

It is difficult to love those who offend us and are hostile to us, but Jesus teaches us that at times love must be unilateral. Jesus tells us to turn the other cheek, to lower our defenses. Jesus is not suggesting a soft passivity of one who does not know how to react, but a positive response and initiative not to close off but to rescue the relationship, loving first, forgiving first. Just as God loved us while we were still in sin.

The love Jesus asks of us is not an abstraction, it is practical, operative. As St. Teresa of Avila says, *Obras son amores y no buenas razones* (Works are loves, and not good reasons), Jesus speaks of the gestures that heal wounds and betoken love—a greeting, lending a hand or a tunic, sharing a piece of bread, forgiving first, loving first.

As bishops, we must strive to love the unlovable with a love that is ever less selective, ever more inclusive. We all wish to enter the kingdom of heaven, but Jesus tells us that unless our righteousness surpasses that of the scribes and Pharisees, we will not enter the kingdom.

In the Gospel, we find some very good and holy Pharisees: Nicodemus, Joseph of Arimathea, Gamaliel, and even the apostle of the Gentiles, Paul of Tarsus.

Yet, the term *Pharisee* has come to mean something negative because of the many controversies they had with Jesus. The Pharisees were often obsessed with man-made laws, whereas Jesus is more concerned with love as the basis for the Law and the prophets. The Pharisees scorned sinners, whereas Jesus sought them like a shepherd seeking the lost sheep. The self-righteous, legalistic Pharisees are quick to attack Jesus for curing a sick person on the Sabbath or for forgiving someone's sins, which the Pharisees called blasphemy.

The Pharisees were always seeking ways to entrap and discredit Jesus. They were arrogant, jealous of power, lovers of money, and more concerned about projecting the right image than about living lives of virtue and service.

There is always a danger of living our religion on the surface, on the outside. Jesus is calling us to embrace his gospel in our hearts, so that we might live his values, his attitudes.

"Let the same mind be in you that was in Christ Jesus, who, though he was in the form of God, did not regard equality with God as something to be exploited, but emptied himself, taking the form of a slave....He humbled himself and became obedient to the point of death—even death on a cross" (Phil 2:5–8).

The only way we can have the sentiments of Jesus in our hearts is by being like the Beloved Disciple who placed his head on the heart of Jesus. We must allow the sentiments of Jesus—his priorities and ideals—to invade our minds and our hearts.

Mary, the first of Jesus's disciples, is always pondering the words and the events in her heart, all the while seeking to embrace the will of God with trust and with love.

As bishops, we cannot afford to live our faith on the surface. We must ponder the word of God in our hearts so that that word can become incarnate in us. We began this retreat reflecting on Jesus's priorities and how we can incorporate his priorities and the *unum necessarium* in our lives.

As we draw near the altar each day, we must be striving to heal any broken relationships that impede us from offering the gifts on the altar. We must first make a gift of ourselves as Mary did.

Anger, competition, envy, and resentments are the thieves that prevent our heart from becoming a temple. Those thieves need to be cast out by Christ cleansing our temple.

At the Eucharist, a deacon calls for the sign of peace, a cantor might announce the number of the hymn, but only the celebrant says the words "Let us pray." When we give this invitation, people want to see that we are supposed to know the territory, to be men of prayer.

When we invite our people to pray with us, it is a great responsibility. We need to model in our life how the disciple should draw near the altar only after seeking to be reconciled with our brothers and sisters. We can preside at the Eucharist only by being men of reconciliation, who always strive to heal broken relationships as the ultimate preparation to offer sacrifice to God.

14

THE *HOW* IS MORE IMPORTANT THAN THE *WHAT*

"Return to me" is the gentle invitation that our God gives us. He is waiting patiently, like the father of the prodigal son, who searched the horizon, waiting and hoping, full of mercy and kindness, slow to anger and full of benevolence.

Spiritual writers often speak of a second calling, a moment when God's grace summons us again. When St. Teresa of Avila encountered the image of the *Ecce Homo* (Behold the man) on the walls of her convent, the sight of Christ's sufferings and humiliation melted her heart and rescued her from a life of mediocrity.

During this holy season of Lent, God's grace calls again and again: "Return to me." We need not fear because ours is a loving God. God's love is unconditional, like a loving father who spoils his children by his indulgence.

Let us overcome all the conditions that we put on our love. We love those who are ours, who are like us, look like us, think like us. We love those who love us and are good to us. We love those who entertain us and flatter us. But God tells us that, when we have a banquet, we should not just invite the beautiful people, we should invite the blind, the lame, and the poor who cannot reciprocate. We must learn to love our priests and people even when they criticize us and judge us, or when they are indifferent and ignore us.

Our God who loves us while we are still in sin is teaching us how to love the same way. The lost sheep, the ungrateful, undisciplined, recalcitrant, stubborn, rebellious sheep, must be the object of our quest and our love. We must invite them unceasingly to return just as our heavenly Father never tires of inviting us: "Return to me." "Be not afraid." "I love you." To be instruments of God's mercy, we need to experience it.

The invitation to rend your hearts and not your garments is an invitation to an interior conversion. Sometimes, we place such importance on externals. In the Gospel for Ash Wednesday where Jesus speaks of the traditional acts of penance—prayer, fasting, and almsgiving—the Lord warns us that we should not perform these acts of penance like the Pharisees who gave great importance to externals, creating a good impression and winning people's praise. For Jesus the *how* is more important that the *what*.

An interior conversion is the goal of our Lent. A contrite and humble heart the Lord will not despise. May the Lord's grace and mercy give us a heart transplant replacing our stony heart with a heart of flesh, a converted heart that weeps for our sins and rejoices in God's mercy.

15

THE LANGUAGE OF LOVE IS HERE AND NOW

In one of Kierkegaard's edifying sermons, he speaks of a gambler who wants to reform his life. He stands in front of a mirror as if speaking to God in his own image. The man said, "Gambling is my sin, I confess. It is destroying my life and the lives of my loved ones. I am repentant. I shall renounce this sin forever. I am so sorry for having offended you my loving God. Tonight will be my last visit to a casino."

The man will continue in his vice. The language of love is here and now. Lent is our acceptable time. The alarm is urgent. We must respond to the cry of the poor right now, and not say, "Come back tomorrow and I shall help you."

The proverbs written centuries before Jesus preached the gospel in Galilee echo the sentiments of the Great Commandment: love of God and love of neighbor go together.

Do not deny help to the one who needs it. Don't make the poor man wait for alms. *Bis dat qui cito dat* (He who gives promptly, gives double).

Do not conflict with your neighbor or plot against him. Do not practice violence.

If you love and help your neighbor, then God offers you his friendship. For God, today is more important than tomorrow. Love is always prepared to act, to reach out to the poor and needy. In the gospel, Jesus never says come back tomorrow. He cures the people who ask. Same-day service like the dry cleaners. Tomorrow is not in Jesus's vocabulary.

We must learn to love right now, to respond to God's grace right now. The reward is enormous. If we are good neighbors to each other, we can enjoy God's friendship.

This is what our vocation is about. Jesus says, "Now I call you friends," but our friendship grows by helping our neighbor, by being good to those in need.

If we are self-centered, narcissistic, selfish people, we risk losing God's friendship.

How can we say we love our God whom we cannot see, if we do not love our neighbor whom we can see?

Do we want to enjoy God's friendship? Then we must learn to love right now, to express our love for God in the concrete and immediate ways that we respond to the needs of those around us.

16

HUMILITY AND LOVE

In America, when someone is appointed bishop, we usually say, "Congratulations. You will never get a bad meal, but no one will ever tell you the truth." Having been so well fed since I became a bishop, I suspect also that people are not telling me the truth.

We usually don't object when people are flattering us and exaggerating our virtues, talents, or eloquence. In the parable of the Pharisee and the publican, the religious leader is congratulating himself for all his good works. As the Spanish *refran* says, *No necesita abuelos, se celebra solo* (It does not need grandparents, it is celebrated alone).

One of the favors that our real friends and our enemies do is to criticize us for our sins and failures. As the Book of Proverbs tells us, "The ear that listens to healthy criticism will be counted among the wise. The one who heeds correction gains understanding. Fear of the Lord is the school of wisdom. Humility comes before glory."

There are times when we need to hear the truth even when it is embarrassing and so many would prefer to deceive us rather than merit our anger.

Criticism can be like cod liver oil, one of the greatest sources of many vitamins, but when I was a child, it was sometimes administered to recalcitrant children as a punishment because it tasted so bad. In the United States, we have an advertisement for Listerine mouthwash that says, "Anything that tastes this bad must be good for you."

As the word of God reminds us, humility must come before glory, or as Jesus says, "He who humbles himself will be exalted." Sometimes, it is our pride and insecurity that makes us so desirous of praise and flattery and so adverse to be corrected or criticized. It is the same lack of humility that makes it so hard to praise the accomplishments of others because we fear that we will be eclipsed by the good deeds of others. The Pharisees saw Jesus as a threat and they hated him.

Let us rejoice in the good deeds and good fortune of our brothers and sisters and lament their failures and humiliations, rather than rejoice over their failures and lament their success. Humility and love are what give value to the most insignificant actions; however, without humility and love, the greatest triumphs are worthless in God's eyes.

17

BE NOT AFRAID

There was once a popular country western song where the father of a young woman is trying to emphasize to the young man who is taking her on a date the importance of bringing his daughter home before midnight. He tells the young man, "I'll be here waiting, just cleaning my shotgun."

I grew up in a world where fear was often used to motivate people. There were great sermons about hell and eternal punishment. Some might say that fear was very effective. Nobody missed Sunday Mass nor ate a hamburger on Friday. After the Council, more emphasis was placed on the mercy and compassion of God.

The theme from today's reading can seem old fashioned, out-of-date. Nobody talks about fear of the Lord. However, there are three hundred references to fear of the Lord in the Bible, and fear of the Lord is the seventh gift of the Holy Spirit. I must confess that fear of the Lord is not the theme of my confirmation homilies, but today's reading from Proverbs (15:30–33) focuses our attention on fear of the Lord.

Fear of the Lord helps us to live the commandments, to live authentic lives of discipleship where there is no contradiction between what we preach and how we live. It is a fear that is not servile but filial. Von Balthasar has a splendid biography of St. Therese where he describes her reverence for her parents and the deep conviction of their unconditional love for her. She would never want to offend them by being ungrateful for their love. Fear of the Lord is the beginning of wisdom, but love is its completion.

Moses removes his sandals before the burning bush in awe of the mystery. Having been in God's presence on Sinai, Moses had to veil his face. We, who are men of God, must perceive the mystery and grandeur of God. We must experience God's holiness and communicate it by our reverence and decorum in celebrating the divine mysteries and preaching the word of God.

Once I was invited to preach in a beautiful old Gothic church. I climbed the many steps to the pulpit, but as I approached the top and was placing my notes on the pulpit, there, where only the preacher could read them, were the words from John's Gospel: "Sir, we would see Jesus." What a responsibility. Kierkegaard says that to preach is a risk because whether the church is full or empty, there is one listener who is unseen, God in heaven.

There was a film called *The Eye in the Sky*. It made me recall the symbol that often appeared in our churches and is on every one-dollar bill: an eye within a triangle, symbolizing the all-seeing eye of God.

Fear of the Lord is being aware that God's loving glance is always on us. Everything that happens in our life is important to our loving God. He is never indifferent. He is always watching us with love.

How often the Gospels contain the mantra "Fear not." We are afraid of the dark, of death, of hunger, poverty, violence. We are afraid of being embarrassed, criticized.

We must renounce those fears. We can be free by trusting in God's love. Our only fear should be to betray such love.

18

CALLED TO BE PASTOR AND FATHER

In 1992, we were celebrating the five hundredth anniversary of Christopher Columbus's arrival to the Virgin Islands—islands that Columbus named in honor of St. Ursula and the eleven thousand virgins. Commemorative stamps to mark Columbus's landing on St. Croix were issued by the United States and Italy, Columbus's native land. The head of the Italian postal services attended the ceremonies on St. Croix and was taken by the natural, unspoiled beauty of the place—white beaches, palm trees, and crystal-clear blue water. He said to me, "Excellency, you have chosen a beautiful place to be a bishop." I said, "I have chosen nothing, the Holy Father sent me here." To which he replied, *Il Papa é infallible* (The pope is infallible).

Many of our priests would be quick to point out that unfortunately, papal infallibility does not extend to the naming of bishops, and they could give us many egregious examples to prove their point. However, today we are most grateful that our Holy Father, Pope Benedict, has wisely named this excellent priest to be our auxiliary bishop. In so doing, the

Holy Father is not naming a stranger, but one of his own collaborators who work closely with him. Msgr. Robert Deeley is a man whose priestly spirituality, pastoral zeal, and keen intellect prepare him well for the office of bishop.

In today's world, the office of bishop is not well understood. One man was quoted as saying the only bishop I know is on my chessboard. Indeed, one of the traditional chess pieces is shaped like a miter and called the bishop. I shall give no mystical interpretation to the diagonal movement of that chess piece. One chess manual urges the reader to use the bishop sparingly, saving him for heroic deeds in the endgame. We are expecting many heroic deeds from our new bishop, and not just in the endgame.

St. Teresa of Avila was a fan of chess and saw in this game a metaphor for the spiritual life. She says that the goal of the spiritual life, like chess, is to capture the king. In our quest to capture the king, the role of the bishop is crucial. One of the most important things the Catholic Church does is to make bishops who can link us to the apostles and to Christ himself, and who allow us to be a eucharistic people. And without the Eucharist, how sad the world would be. I know that many here would adhere to the cry of the Martyrs of Abitinae, who told Diocletian, *Sine Domenico non possumus* (Without Sunday Eucharist we could not survive).

Christ founded the Church on the apostles, the first bishops. Mostly, they were simple fishermen, ill prepared for the task that Jesus gave them. They became vessels of clay-bearing treasures, who carried the good news of the gospel to the ends of the earth, witnessing to the truth of their preaching by gladly shedding their blood in witness to the gospel.

All of us are acquainted with Leonardo da Vinci's portrait of the Last Supper. Today's Gospel presents St. Luke's portrait of the last breakfast. Our feckless fishermen apostles had toiled the whole night and caught nothing, but now the risen Lord had arrived, and everything changed for the better. Peter hastened to put on all his clothes and then jumped into the water because the Beloved Disciple had declared, "It is the Lord!"

When Peter reached the shore, he found Jesus was cooking. This is the only instance where the Scriptures hint at Jesus's culinary prowess. Obviously, the Blessed Mother gave Jesus a few tips in the kitchen. Certainly, Jesus had learned from his mother that the fresher the fish, the better. (In Fall River, a Portuguese housewife will routinely ask the fishmonger what time the fish was caught.) The first thing Jesus says to Peter is, "Bring some of the fish you have just caught!"

Peter throws himself back into the sea and swims toward the boat. He then drags the nets to land with 153 fish, and still the net did not break. Scholars have produced many volumes speculating on the mystical meaning of the number 153. Some have related the number to various parts of the Torah. St. Augustine, however, surmised that 153 is the triangular of 17. In other words, if you add up all the numbers decreasing from 17 you will reach 153.

But do you know what I think it means? Not to doubt St. Augustine, I think it means that there were 153 fish in the net. My dad was a great angler, and when he returned from a fishing expedition, he could always tell you how many fish he caught, at what time, and how much each one weighed. I often joke that Peter was a lousy fisherman, and that he caught nothing unless Jesus was right there telling him, "Cast the net here, now!" But, Peter was a real fisherman and would have kept track of how many fish he caught.

At the beginning of the Gospel after the first miraculous draft of fishes, Peter says to Jesus, "Depart from me, Lord, for I am a sinful man." Jesus does not depart, but instead calls Peter to be "a fisher of people." Approximately three years later, at the end of the Gospel, comes today's story. It is déjà vu all over again—another miraculous draft of fishes and St. Peter's profound sense of unworthiness. Yet, just as at the beginning of the Gospel, Jesus invites Peter again saying, "Follow me." Spiritual writers often speak of a second calling, which is a profound grace and deepening of our own personal conversion. Our response to the first call can often be romantic, self-seeking, and shallow. The response to a second call is characterized by purification, greater humility, and a greater dependence upon God's grace. Today's Gospel is definitely Peter's second call.

If the first time Jesus called Peter, he felt unworthy, imagine how Peter felt now, having denied that he even knew Jesus. What is worse is that Peter denied knowing Jesus, not to a soldier with a long knife, but to a waitress with an attitude. That bonfire by the shore of the Sea of Galilee is a reminder of the bonfire in the courtyard of the high priest where Peter denies the Lord, hears the cock crow, and where Jesus turns and looks at Peter in the face. The Gospel records that Peter went out and wept bitterly. The sight of the Master's face bathed in blood melted Peter's heart.

Peter had done what all of us try to do at some point in our live, and that is he tried to follow Jesus at a safe distance, but he discovered that that is not possible. The invitation to follow is an invitation to follow up close, to embrace the cross.

At the last breakfast, Peter is standing before the risen Lord. Peter is soaking wet after having jumped into the sea to swim ashore and then again after Jesus sends him back for fresh fish. Peter was wet, cold, tired, but mostly, he was ashamed of the three times he denied Jesus. Jesus gives him the opportunity to erase those denials, asking Peter three times, "Do you love me?"

St. John of the Cross says that at the end of our life, we will be examined in love. That's all that really matters in today's Gospel: Peter is being examined in love. At Caesarea

Philippi, Peter makes his confession of faith; at the sea of Tiberius, Peter makes his confession of love.

The triple denial of Jesus by Peter destroyed the close relationship that Peter had with his Master. Peter was then absent from some of the most significant events of the Gospel: the royal lifting up of Jesus on the cross (*Jesus Nazarenus Rex Iudaeorum*); the foundation of Jesus's new family of God (Behold thy mother, behold thy son); and the gift of the Spirit (*emisit Spiritum*). All these events have been marked by the presence of the Beloved Disciple and the absence of Peter. The denials must be overcome, and in the rhythmic repetition of the question "Do you love me?" there is a hint of an accusation: "You once denied me....Are you sure of your relationship to me now?"

Peter is embarrassed, but his honest response led to Christ's acceptance of Peter's confession of love and the establishment of a new relationship. Peter is charged to shepherd and feed Jesus's flock. Peter's identification with the Good Shepherd must prepare him to make his own the words of Jesus: "I have come that they may have love and have it more abundantly." "I lay down my life for my sheep." "I have other sheep....And there shall be one flock and one shepherd."

Peter's love for the Lord must manifest itself in the way that he loves Christ's flock, the Church. His profession of love is followed by a solemn prediction about Peter's future, about laying down his life for the flock. Peter's commitment to the way of the Good Shepherd also associates him with the meaning of Christ's death. For Peter's unconditional acceptance of his role as shepherd of the sheep of Jesus will also lead to the glorification of God in his self-gift in love unto death, when a rope will be tied around him and he will be led where he would rather not go.

After examining Peter in love and charging him to feed the flock and to lay down his life, Jesus then invites Peter once again with those words that echo through the history of the Church: "Follow me." The invitation is to follow Jesus, not as Peter did when he fled from Gethsemane and tried to follow at a safe distance, but instead Jesus invites Peter to follow up close in unswerving discipleship all the rest of his days.

Jesus is teaching us that all ministry is about love, about laying down one's life for the flock, and that ministry is born out of a deep friendship with the risen Lord. Peter and the apostles lived out their vocation feeding Christ's flock and confirming the faith, making the Good Shepherd's love present to God's people. The gifts of ministry do not end with the apostles but have been passed on by the laying on of hands and the gifts of the Spirit.

Today, in our presence, Robert Deeley will receive the same ordination and share in the apostle's role. Jesus is calling this man to follow him and to be a shepherd after his own heart.

By this sacrament the power and love of the Good Shepherd and the gifts of the Spirit are made available to believers of every age. Without bishops in the lineage of the apostles, there would be no priests, no magisterium, no power to forgive sins, and no possibility of Eucharist. That is why the Church sees the ordinations of bishops as the key to our identity as Catholics. It is the way that Christ's loving plan is continued throughout history. Our bishops are ordained by bishops to fulfill the mission Christ has given to teach, to sanctify, to lead.

The ordination ceremony speaks to us about the meaning of this sacrament. The rite calls for a ring to be placed on the new bishop's finger. It is a wedding ring. Indeed, the Spanish word for the bishop's ring is *esposa*, which means "bride." The bishop represents Christ, the divine bridegroom, and is to love the Church entrusted to him as his bride. The bishop's ordination contains many phrases that represent this aspect of being wedded to the Church. The bishop, like the bridegroom and father of the family, must have a special love for God's people.

Bishop Elect Robert, the homily in the ritual and the questions directed to the candidate for ordination speak to us about your role. You are told "to pray always," for and with your people, and as a father and brother to love all those whom God places in your care. Love priests and deacons, who share with you the ministry of Christ. Love the poor and infirm, strangers and the homeless, and seek out the sheep who stray. And, most importantly, you must guard the deposit of the faith entire and incorrupt as handed down by the apostles. You are to bear witness to the truth of the gospel. Remember Christ's words to the apostles: "Whoever listens to you listens to me, and whoever rejects you, rejects me, and whoever rejects me rejects the One who sent me."

Along with a miter, a wedding crown, you will be given a staff, the bishop's crosier. You are to be an icon of the Good Shepherd. Be like the Good Shepherd who knows his sheep and is known by them, and who does not hesitate to "lay down his life for them."

You will be ordained bishop in the apostolic succession by the same laying on of hands that ordained that cloud of witnesses: Matthias and Timothy, John Chrysostom, Patrick and Augustine, Boniface and Denis, Charles Borromeo, John Fisher, John Carroll, Jean-Louis Lefevre de Cheverus, Oliver Plunkett, John Newman, József Mindszenty, Fulton Sheen, Richard Cushing, James Walsh, Oscar Romero, and Francois Van Thuan, bishops in the apostolic succession called to be one in the college of bishops in union with Peter, to proclaim the Catholic faith with one voice, to be witnesses of the resurrection, to be spiritual fathers and shepherds.

Bishop Robert, whenever you look back on this day, recall the charge of Paul and Timothy:

> I remind you to stir into flame the gift of God that you have through the imposition of my hands. For God did not give us a spirit of cowardice but rather of power and love and self-control. Bear your share of hardship for the gospel with the strength that comes from God. (2 Tim 6–8, NABRE)

And remember always that your ministry is above all a call to follow Christ. You responded generously forty years ago by embracing a vocation to the priesthood. Today is a second call. Like Peter, you are being called to a deeper conversion, to a vocation of love and service. We commend your ministry to the loving care of Mary, the mother of the divine Shepherd, that through her intercession and the grace of this ordination God may grant you a heart according to the heart of Christ who came not to be served but to serve and who lay down his life for the flock.

Episcopal Ordination of Bishop Robert Deeley,
January 4, 2013

19

AMBASSADOR OF CHRIST

Dear brothers and sisters in the Lord, what a joy to be here today! We thought we were coming for the ordination of Archbishop Paul Russell, but this is actually his mother's birthday party. Congratulations to you, Mrs. Russell, and thank you for the gift of your son to the priesthood and the Church.

We welcome the family and friends that have come from the four corners of the earth to be a part of this great celebration. In a very special way, I want to greet the co-consecrators, Archbishop Allen Vigneron of Detroit, a dear friend of Archbishop Russell and a friend of ours; we're so glad to have him here today. We are also joined by Archbishop Leo Cushley of Edinburgh, who gave us a nonalcoholic toast at the festive meal today.

We are also honored and delighted to be joined by his Eminence Metropolitan Methodios of Boston from the Greek Orthodox Church, who is representing His Holiness the Ecumenical Patriarch of Constantinople. The Metropolitan Methodios is a great friend of the archdiocese and has spent much time in Turkey and the Fener in his duties as metropolitan. We are so happy that he could be here today.

Also, as the monsignor did before he read the bull, we gracefully recognize the presence of our two new auxiliary bishops, Bishop-elect Mark O'Connell and Bishop-elect Robert Reed.

St. Paul uses the term *ambassador* for Christ twice in his epistles—in Second Corinthians and in Ephesians. Today, we gather in this Cathedral of the Holy Cross to participate in the consecration of a man who is being called to be an ambassador for Christ, to be an ambassador for the Vicar of Christ, and to go to Turkey to do this.

Pope Francis holds up for us the model of holiness in the diplomatic service in the person of Pope John XXIII. In fact, as I said to Paul, all the stars are lining up for today's feast. This year, June 3, is the Feast of the Sacred Heart. It is also the anniversary of the death of your predecessor as nuncio to Turkey, Angelo Giuseppe Roncalli, the future Pope John XXIII. By rights, today should be his feast day because normally the day a saint dies is commemorated as the feast day; but in the case of Pope John, he was assigned October 11 as his feast day—the date of the opening of the Second Vatican Council.

As fate would have it, today is also the anniversary of the death of a friend of mine, the Capuchin Bishop Luigi Padovese, who was the vicar apostolic of Anatolia, Turkey. He was beheaded six years ago today, on June 3, 2010. All of this is a stark reminder of the many challenges for the Church in Turkey and the importance of the mission you are about to undertake as an ambassador for Christ.

It was in 1934 that Pope John was named apostolic delegate to Turkey in Greece. It was a very difficult assignment, and he was not officially recognized by the government. Nevertheless, his presence in that part of the world proved to be such a blessing after the Second World War broke out; in his role as apostolic delegate, Pope St. John was instrumental in saving the lives of thousands of Jews and of convincing the Allied nations to allow food to be shipped to Greece, where the population was starving to death due to the war.

For Pope St. John, his work as a papal representative was a true ministry. He put a sign on the inside of his office door where he could see it, that said, *Pastor et Pater*. He saw that as his role to be a shepherd and a father. His inspiration was not someone like Metternich or the great treatises of international diplomacy. He always found his inspiration in the tenets of the gospel and saw his role as shepherd and father.

After many years as apostolic delegate, to the surprise of the world, Angelo Roncalli was named to one of the most prestigious diplomatic posts as nuncio to Paris. It was reported that his nomination came about because the nuncio who was supposed to go to Paris fell sick. When Angelo Roncalli was told that he was being named nuncio, he commented, *Ubi deficient equi, trottant aselli* (Where there are no horses to gallop, the donkey will trot along).

My favorite story from those years of Pope John as nuncio in Paris concerns his role as the dean of the diplomatic corps. The Congress of Vienna established that ordinarily the papal nuncio is the dean of the diplomats, carrying with that post many ceremonial and social responsibilities. Hence the venerable archbishop had to go to many cocktail parties and banquets.

On one such occasion, the future Pope John was seated across the table from a beautiful young woman wearing a very abbreviated Parisian outfit. All the eyes were upon the nuncio. Realizing this, the saint picked an apple out of a bowl of fruit that was on the table and offered it to the young lady saying, "Mademoiselle, it was only after Eve ate the apple that she realized she was naked."

Archbishop Paul, we pray that Pope St. John XXIII will be a great inspiration and model for your ministry, and we pray that the good Pope John will intercede as you fulfill the same role as an ambassador for Christ and representative of Pope Francis, bringing his *tenerezza* and *vicinanza* (his tenderness and closeness) to the people of Turkey.

Pope Francis is aware of the many hardships and dangers in your way of life. In addressing the nuncios of the world, the Holy Father describes your life as nomadic—going from one country to another, each with its differences and challenges. Like the Son of Man who, though the foxes have their dens and the birds of the air have their nests, has nowhere to lay his head.

The Holy Father talks of the mortification of carrying a suitcase, not being able to put down roots, living as a perpetual pilgrim. Quoting Pope Paul from his days as *Sostituto*, Pope Francis recalled that the papal representative is someone truly aware that he is bringing Christ with him "as a precious good to communicate, to proclaim and to represent."

Pope Francis says that your life as a papal diplomat demands a detachment from self, and a familiarity with Jesus Christ that is your daily nourishment and that originates in your own memory of that first encounter with him. Familiarity. Being on familiar terms with Jesus Christ in prayer, in the eucharistic celebration, and in the service of charity.

As a nuncio, you are to be a pastor. Your role is to encourage, to be a minister of communion and mercy.

Today marks the day of a special vocation. You are called to the episcopate to enhance your ability to make the pastoral love of the Good Shepherd more visible in your ministry in the service of the Holy Father and the Church.

The selecting of the apostles is one of the most significant acts in Jesus's public life. He went into the hills where he spent the whole night praying to the Father, and when it was day, he called his disciples and chose from them twelve that he named apostles.

These Twelve are called to have a personal relationship with Jesus. He wants them to be his companions. They share the life he leads, with him they constitute a community, which is much more like that of a father and a family than that of teacher and disciples. They are with Jesus throughout his earthly life so that they might be direct witnesses of his words and his actions, and later on, of his resurrection.

The apostles are considered the foundation of the Church. In the Book of Revelation, we read, "The wall of the city had twelve foundations, and on them the twelve names of the twelve apostles of the Lamb" (Rev 21:14). As the patriarchs were the fathers of the twelve tribes of the chosen people of the Old Testament, so the twelve apostles were the foundation of the new people of God.

Pope Clement, who reigned from the year AD 92 to 101, speaking of apostolic succession stated,

> And so the Apostles, after receiving their orders and being fully convinced by the resurrection of our Lord Jesus Christ and assured by God's word, went out in the confidence of the Holy Spirit to preach the good news that God's kingdom was about to come. They preached in country and city, and appointed their first converts, after testing them by the Spirit, to be the bishops and deacons of future believers.

And now, Paul, you will be part of this apostolic succession by the laying on of hands. Immediately after the homily, you will be questioned in the presence of the people of God on your resolve to uphold the faith and to discharge the following duties—the promises betoken the areas of grave responsibility that accrue to the ordained.

Preaching the gospel with constancy and fidelity is one of the first duties of the bishop. In doing so, you must pass on entire and uncorrupt the deposit of the faith.

A bishop must also strive to build the unity in the Church. And very significantly in this Year of Mercy, you are called upon to be a father to the poor, to be welcoming and merciful to those in need, to strangers and to all in need, and like the Good Shepherd, to seek out the sheep who stray and gather them to the Lord's fold.

And finally, the Church asks you to resolve to pray without ceasing for the Holy People of God.

In fulfilling these duties, you shall become an icon of the Good Shepherd.

Being ordained on the Feast of the Sacred Heart, our new archbishop has chosen the motto of Blessed John Henry Cardinal Newman, who was named a cardinal at age seventy-eight, and chose *Cor ad cor loquitur* (Heart speaks to heart), as his cardinalatial motto. It is a beautiful phrase lifted from the writings of St. Francis de Sales.

The Greeks refer to St. John the Apostle as *epistemios*, "He who rested his head on Christ's heart." Let Christ's heart speak to yours, make his sentiments your own so that you too will be a reflection of Christ's pastoral love. Learn from him who is meek and humble of heart. Be consumed by thirst for souls and the desire to rescue that lost sheep who has strayed the farthest. The priority of the Good Shepherd was the one lost sheep who was farthest away. Pope Francis reminds us of Jesus's priorities when he tells us to go to the periphery.

The Prophet Ezekiel speaks to us about the shepherd who gathers the scattered and binds up their wounds and heals the sick. In Romans, St. Paul reminds us how Christ died for us while we were still sinners and in this, he proves his love and pours that love into our hearts.

This Gospel for the Feast of the Sacred Heart is so appropriate. Luke, the Gospel of mercy, portrays the joy of the Good Shepherd as he finds the lost sheep and sets it on his shoulders with joy and invites us to rejoice with him because he found his lost sheep.

Paul, as you assume the vocation of apostle during this Jubilee of Mercy, may the mercy of the Good Shepherd be the constant theme of your service to the Lord and his Church, and may being a minister of God's mercy bring you much joy.

And may Mary, the Mother of the Divine Shepherd (*Mater Divini Pastoris*), protect you, guide you, and help you to have a heart like her Son. And may your heart always speak with the Sacred Heart, *cor ad cor loquitur*.

Episcopal Ordination of Archbishop Paul Russell,
June 3, 2016

20

ONLY LOVE IS CONVINCING

First, on behalf of my brother bishops in the United States, I wish to thank Father Peter Harman and the faculty and staff of the Pontifical North American College for their excellent work in forming young men for the Catholic priesthood in this extraordinary setting, allowing our seminarians to experience the catholicity of our Church and to be close to the ministry of the Holy Father, the successor of St. Peter.

I congratulate the ordinands and thank and congratulate their families and pastors who have nurtured their vocations with prayers, their good example, and encouragement.

What a privilege it is to have this ordination in one of the most sacred spots in Christendom, in this magnificent basilica built on the tomb of Peter, the rock on whom Christ has built his church. And in the shadow of St. Michael looking down on us from the Castel San Angelo on this Feast of Michaelmas, like the great archangel may you say, "I will serve"; like Gabriel, may you be a messenger of the good news; and like Raphael, a healer.

I am reminded today of my own ordination to the diaconate, which took place in the crypt of the Basilica of the National Shrine of the Immaculate Conception in Washington, DC. There were many ordinands from many religious communities that were clustered around the Catholic University of America. Only the religious attended; the diaconate ceremony was part of the *disciplina arcani,* like the initiation ceremony for the Knights of Columbus, so our families were not invited. It is grand to have so many relatives of our ordinands here in St. Peter's.

When I was a deacon, I had been told that I was going to be a missionary on Easter Island, but during my diaconate it was determined that there were enough big stone heads on Easter Island and that I should be stationed in Washington to work with the newly arrived and underserved Hispanic population. Spiritually, I identify with those seven men ordained by the Twelve, to serve the Hellenic Christians living in Jerusalem.

The Acts of the Apostles describes the selection and ordination of the first deacons. They were seven men filled with faith and the Holy Spirit, but reading between the lines, we can suppose that these seven men were ordained not only because of their spiritual qualities but also because they spoke Greek.

Allow me to offer a public service announcement at this point in support of Hispanic ministry in our country. More than half of Americans under the age of thirty, and 70 percent of those under age eighteen are Hispanic. Those statistics, which will likely increase in the years ahead as Hispanics continue to arrive and to have children and establish large families, call for a pastoral response. So, if you do not yet speak Spanish, try to learn the language. It is easier than Greek.

There is something very original about the diaconate. Unlike the priest and the bishop, the deacon has no clear

Jewish or pagan counterpart. The glory of this specific office lies in its being born of the distinctive *diakonia* quality that Christ modeled and communicated to the ministry of the Church he founded.

Jesus presents himself as the one who has come to serve. He is the Suffering Servant, he is meek and humble of heart, he is born in a barn and buried in a borrowed grave. Jesus wants his followers to have the same spirit of service and humility.

Sometimes, we relate the deacons to the Levites of the Old Testament, and although there are some similarities in the liturgical roles, the vocation of the deacon is really very different. In the parable of the Good Samaritan, the reference to the Levite's behavior is not flattering, for he encounters the brutally beaten man by the side of the road and turns and walks away. Possibly he feared incurring ritual impurity by touching a corpse, but he did not bother to draw near to determine if the man was still alive or not. The Levite and the priest of the parable of the Good Samaritan saw their role as primarily liturgical and ceremonial and therefore did not feel compelled to involve themselves with the man left half dead by the side of the road.

I would remind you that as deacons you have sacred functions in the liturgy, but the very first role of the deacon was to care for the material needs of widows and orphans. In the life of a priest and deacon there can be no dichotomy between our cultic role and the humble service we must give, as in washing the feet of our brothers and sisters. The towel should be as emblematic as the stole for our priests and deacons, whose humble service must reflect the humble and loving service of the Good Shepherd. Part of our task is to connect the works of mercy with the Eucharist. It is not by accident that the washing of the feet of the apostles takes place in the context of the first Eucharist.

St. Mother Teresa saw so clearly the connection between the Eucharist and the works of mercy. Every time she opened a new house, she would say there would be a new tabernacle where Jesus will be adored and next to the crucifix in every chapel, she put a sign with the words *I thirst*. From there, each day St. Mother Teresa's sisters go forth to carry God's mercy to the abandoned, the suffering, the sick, to Jesus in a distressing disguise.

As a young priest at the Centro Católico in Washington, I ran a program in Spanish to prepare deacons. Not all pastors are anxious to have deacons assigned to their parishes. The permanent diaconate had just been restored by the Second Vatican Council and some priests felt that the deacons were a threat to their authority and ministry, and they offered much resistance to having deacons.

This manifested itself in one comic circumstance when the newly minted deacon in his first liturgical appearance asked for the priest's blessing before proclaiming the Gospel. In what might have been a Freudian slip, the pastor blessed the deacon with the words for the blessing of incensea: *Ab illo benedicaris in cujus honorem cremaberis*, which means, "May you be blessed by him in whose honor you will burn." That's telling the deacons where to go.

Actually, the blessing of the deacon is a beautiful prayer, full of meaningful challenge. Before proclaiming the Gospel, the deacon kneels before the celebrant and asks for the blessing, and the priest blesses him with the words, *Dominus sit in corde tuo et labiis tuis ut digne et competenter annunties Evangelium suum. In nomine Patris et Filii et Spiritus Sancti. Amen* (May the Lord be in your heart and on your lips so that you may worthily [and competently] proclaim the Gospel in the name of the Father and of the Son and of the Holy Spirit. Amen).

In the first reading today, Jeremiah writes, "The Lord touched my lips and declares: see how I placed my words in your mouth" (Jer 1:9). As deacons you are ministers of the word of God. The Lord must be in your heart and on your lips.

The blessing invokes God's favor that you may worthily and competently (the competence part is lost in the translation) proclaim the gospel. Your worthiness depends on your ongoing conversion and fidelity to grace. Your life, as today's Gospel says, is to bear fruit that will remain. The fruits you will produce will be an advertisement for the gospel and make you worthy to announce the good news.

But as the Latin form of the blessing reminds us, you need to be competent to proclaim the gospel. Don't bore the people to death. Show them the beauty of Christ's gospel and show them that you love them, that you are a friend ready to lay down your life for them. People will listen only to those who love them. Brilliant arguments and eloquent syllogisms can help, but if you are not a spiritual father—a missionary ready to sacrifice all—your message will not be heard. When people feel that you care about them and their well-being, they will accept your message. Only love is convincing; only holiness is convincing.

We have to love God's people even when they don't love us. [As noted earlier,] I have always liked the story about the Curé of Ars, who was asked by a group of disgruntled parishioners to celebrate a Mass once a week for a special intention. After several weeks, the saint was getting curious and said to the people, "Obviously, we have not yet received what we are praying for, since you are still asking for the Mass. What is it that we are praying for, what is the special intention?" The people answered, "We are praying that the bishop will send you to another parish." The people of Ars were not always happy to hear what their pastor said, but they became convinced how much he loved them and that allowed them to change their lives and embrace lives of discipleship.

In his retreat for priests during this Year of Mercy, Pope Francis notes that at the end of Mark's Gospel, the disciples went forth and preached everywhere while the Lord worked with them and confirmed the word through accompanying signs. The Holy Father gives us the image of the Lord who collaborates with the apostles and confirms the word with signs that are works of mercy, curing the sick and casting out evil spirits.

Your preaching of the word needs to be confirmed by works of mercy. Indeed, you are being ordained deacons during this Jubilee of Mercy. Your task is to help promote the culture of mercy in our faith communities. That is why deacons were created.

Have a special love for the poor and the sick. Be a friend of immigrants, strangers, and prisoners. In *Evangelii Gaudium*, Pope Francis points out that often the poor do not receive the pastoral care that they need. We often respond to people's material needs but forget about their spiritual hunger for the word of God and the sacraments.

Do not allow Lazarus to be invisible; remember that the priorities of Jesus in the gospel are the little ones, the poor, the sick, the blind, the lame, the lepers, the prostitutes, the tax collectors, and the lost sheep. They are the protagonists of the gospel of mercy. A deacon is a minister at the table, a minister of the word, and a minister of charity.

As minister at the table, you are the waiter. The waiter is not the center of attention. He is a man who is there to serve, to provide hospitality. We are called to make people feel at home in church. Pope Francis once spoke about a parish secretary in Buenos Aires who drove people away from the church. People called her "the tarantula." The deacon is to be a man of hospitality. One author wrote that all our priests and deacons and parish staff should be sent to a course given by the Four Seasons Hotel, to train them in the art of hospitality. He noted that, as it is, some seemed to have been trained by the U.S. Postal Service.

You must work to make people feel welcomed and work to make their experience of the Church uplifting. Work to make the liturgy beautiful so that people can experience a community of faith and joy and glimpse God's beauty. In *Evangelii Gaudium*, Pope Francis speaks about the *via pulchritudinis*, as a privileged instrument of evangelization.

Love the Eucharist, make it beautiful. Teach people to pray so that they can worship our God. In the Eucharist, Jesus the Deacon and High Priest makes a gift of himself so that we can be nourished for our mission, and so that we can make a gift of ourselves to God. Pope St. John Paul II always said human fulfillment is only achieved by making a gift of ourselves.

Today, you men are making a gift of yourselves to God and his people in a life of obedience, chastity, and prayerfulness. May Mary, the Mother of the Divine Shepherd guide and protect you so that you might be worthy and competent messengers of the gospel. And may God who has begun this good work in you bring it to fulfillment.

Diaconate Ordination at Saint Peter's Basilica,
Rome, September 30, 2016

21

THE LORD OF THE SABBATH

An outspoken widow, Anna Flannigan, was a priest's housekeeper in Pittsburg. One day, she took a phone call from one of the friends of the pastor, who was calling to inquire about the pastor's convalescence following a surgery. He asked, "Is Father Jim back at work yet?" Without missing a beat, Anna replied, "Well, if you call saying Mass on Sunday work, I guess he is."

If we are defined by what we do, certainly in the minds of our people the priest is the Sunday guy. In fact, some people may harbor the belief that during the other six days of the week Father is playing golf, or watching daytime television, or visiting the Mohegan Sun Casino. Although that is a very unfair and inaccurate characterization of the life of a priest, it does not take away from the fact that it is on Sunday that a priest is truly living out his priesthood to the fullest. The Lord's Day is also Father Jim's day.

It is the Gospel of Luke that speaks to us most about Jesus and the Sabbath. In fact, there are twice as many mentions of the Sabbath in Luke as in any of the other Gospels.

It is significant that seven of Jesus's miracles are performed on the Sabbath. Jesus raises the question after curing the man with dropsy: "Is it lawful to cure on the Sabbath?" (cf. Luke 6:1–5; 14:1–11). Jesus answers the question by saying, "I desire mercy, not sacrifice....I am the Lord of the Sabbath." The scribes and Pharisees wanted to kill Jesus because they thought the holy day was more important than the One who made it holy.

Jesus used the Sabbath. He made it a day of mercy, in his preaching and in his miracles, to deliver people from bondage. He preached the good news and announced the jubilee year. He gave physical sight to a few, but spiritual sight to many. He did not release anyone from physical prisons but freed many from spiritual captivity.

Luke shows us how Jesus establishes his ministry on the Sabbath and proclaims a jubilee of mercy. Here we see Jesus's predilection for the poor, his love for sinners, and also his love for prayer. These three themes are woven throughout the Lukan Gospel that is used in this year's cycle. It is so fitting because it is our Jubilee Year of Mercy, and Luke's Gospel is the Gospel of mercy.

The Gospel shows us how Jesus, our High Priest, is of course in church on the Sabbath preaching the word of God.

Almost without exception, my dear brothers, I know that our Sabbath finds you at the altar and in the pulpit feeding your people with the word of life and the bread from heaven.

Chapter 6 of the wonderful book *Rebuilt* is titled, "It's the Weekend, Stupid." There, Father Michael White and Tom Corcoran explain how they renewed the Church of the Nativity starting with the weekend experience. They quote Pope St. John Paul II, who said, "Among the many activities of a parish, none is as vital or as community-forming as the Sunday celebration of the Lord's Day."

Three times in the Gospels, Jesus calls himself the Lord of the Sabbath. Jesus inaugurates his public ministry on the Sabbath by announcing a year of grace.

This jubilee year was to be a Sabbath year. Slaves and indentured servants were to be set free, debts were to be forgiven, the fields should lay fallow, and the mercy of God would be made manifest. Our Year of Mercy is about the forgiveness of debts.

In the Bible, the jubilee year also reflects God's desire that there be a just distribution of the earth's resources. In a world where one hundred individuals possess half the wealth on the planet, the Jubilee reflects the Catholic social teaching that all wealth has a social mortgage.

The Jubilee year must be a time when we—priests and the people of God—focus on the social teaching of the Church, which is a constitutive part of evangelization, as Pope Paul VI stated so clearly. Sacred Scripture is a mirror of how mercy is expressed in its concreteness. The Bible highlights the reality of mercy in its tangible and visible expression.

In the papal document announcing the extraordinary Jubilee of Mercy, *Misericordiae Vultus*, Pope Francis describes the reason for his great convocation to the Holy Year by starting with the state of our world:

> Let us open our eyes and see the misery of the world, the wounds of our brothers and sisters who are denied their dignity, and let us recognize that we are compelled to heed their cry for help. (no. 15)

What is striking about all these Sabbath and jubilee laws in the Scriptures is the way in which worship and giving of offerings are intimately connected with acts of justice, compassion, and mercy. Such acts of justice and sharing are grounded again and again in the memory of who the Israelites were and what God had done for them: "Remember that you were a slave in Egypt."

Indeed, there are two different versions of the Sabbath commandment: one rooted in the story of Creation; the other in the exodus story. Sabbath rest is built into creation and so applies to all humans and all non-human creatures. The Sabbath is a sign of God's special covenant with Israel. God's resting on the Sabbath after six days of creation invites reflection on the mystery of the eternal God who is beyond time and yet enters time out of love for the world. In the story of Creation, God both hallows and makes holy the Sabbath day and blesses it.

The Deuteronomic Sabbath is rooted in the exodus experience of Israel: "Remember that you were slaves in the land of Egypt, and the LORD your God brought you out from there with a mighty hand and an outstretched arm; therefore the LORD your God commanded you to keep the Sabbath day" (Deut 5:15). In other words, observing the Sabbath—doing the practice of resting from work and gathering in worship—serves to generate memory. We remember who we were and who we are; we were slaves, and now we are free. We remember what God did for us: the Lord brought us out of slavery. We remember our core identity; we are God's own people.

The Sabbath becomes an antidote to the spiritual amnesia that disorients modern people when they forget about God. The practice of Sabbath serves to jog our memories back to the truth of our authentic identity and purpose as the people of God. This has implications for understanding the role of liturgy and the practice within worship. Liturgy creates and shapes our memory, which, in turn, shapes our core commitments, actions, and beliefs.

This Year of Mercy is our jubilee, our Sabbath year that affords us the opportunity to live the social gospel of the Church more intensely: preaching and practicing the works of mercy; fostering the gospel values in our society; and promoting the dignity of every human person from conception to natural death, the importance of family, the common good of society, and the centrality of reconciliation and forgiveness.

As Jesus proclaims a jubilee Sabbath year, he describes his mission as announcing the good news to the poor, to liberate captives, and give sight to the blind. This provides us, as Jesus's priests, with a template for our task as jubilee priests in the Year of Mercy. In setting our pastoral priorities and plans and strategies of evangelization, let us try to bring the good news to the poor! Jesus's first pastoral priority!

In the apostolic letter *Evangelii Gaudium*, Pope Francis issues the following challenge:

> Since this Exhortation is addressed to members of the Catholic Church, I want to say, with regret, that the worst discrimination which the poor suffer is the lack of spiritual care. The great majority of the poor have a special openness to the faith; they need God and we must not fail to offer them his friendship, his blessings, his word, the celebration of the sacraments and a journey of growth and maturity in the faith. Our preferential option for the poor must mainly translate into a privileged and preferential religious care. (no. 200)

In the Catholic Church, we are very good about trying to help people in their physical needs, but the Holy Father urges us to strive to bring a special pastoral care to the poor, those who because of age, infirmity, language, homelessness, or legal status are cut off from the pastoral care and sacramental ministry of our Church.

As both Sabbath and jubilee men, our task is to bring liberation to those who are oppressed and captive. Today, some of the worst forms of oppression and captivity are the addictions that destroy peoples' lives: heroin, alcohol, and pornography. Drug overdose is the leading cause of accidental deaths in the United States, with 47,000 lethal overdoses last year; in Massachusetts there are almost three times as many deaths from overdoses as from automobile accidents. I know that you are seeing this in your parishes.

May the Year of Mercy be a time for us to be a field hospital for these families. We are so grateful for the work of Father Joe White and for all the parishes supporting 12-step programs. We are seeing an epidemic and part of our Sabbath year must be responding to this human crisis in our midst. As men of mercy, we must be present to our people in their suffering. So many people need spiritual healing, to be freed from the bondage of sin. We have that power to heal in confession and outside.

The jubilee man also brings sight to the blind. So many of our people are immersed in darkness of religious illiteracy. Our Catholic people urgently need faith formation. We must not waste any opportunity to announce the good news both in season and out of season. We must help people to see that being a Catholic is a way of life that includes both an individual vocation—every priest is a vocation director—and the sharing in a common mission to build a civilization of love, and to care for our common home. Christ is the light of the world, and our task is to bring that light to those who are suffering in darkness. If not enough sunlight can cause SAD (Seasonal Affective Disorder), then being deprived of Christ's light and friendship engenders an existential sadness; Christ tells us to let our light shine before men, and so lead them in the divine light.

When I was a child, the government thought people were so dumb that they would not be able to distinguish between real butter and oleomargarine, so they passed a law that the manufacturers of margarine could not color the margarine yellow. It was sold with a capsule of yellow dye inside a plastic package of white margarine. After purchase, the capsule was broken inside the package and then kneaded to distribute the dye and turn the lardlike substance into a golden yellow: "I can't believe it's not butter." It wasn't until 1955 that the artificial coloring laws were repealed, and margarine could be sold for the first time colored like butter. Still, I remember many a time when I was given the important responsibility to color the margarine. My mother used to call this "putting the sunshine" into the butter. It was one of the chores we did to earn that quarter allowance.

Many have commented that our task is to change God from a Sunday acquaintance into an everyday friend. That capsule of golden dye that is the Sabbath must be broken open and distributed to the rest of the week. Jesus is the Lord of the Sabbath, and he tells us that the Sabbath is for us. The celebration of the Eucharist—the word, the sacrament, and the community of faith—are what give such power to the Sabbath experience.

Our task as the Sunday guys—men of the Sabbath and men of the Sabbath Year of Jubilee—is to change the white oleomargarine into golden butter to put the sunshine back in.

On the Sabbath, God makes creation holy. The Sabbath is holy and the priest as Sabbath man is called to a life of holiness. Real holiness is never an abstract, pie in the sky, or angelic state. In fact, holiness is never realized separate from the stuff of our ordinary daily lives. We are always being called to be patient, generous, attentive, caring, compassionate, and forgiving at this moment, with these people whom I see in front of me. Holiness is always a matter of the now, and how we respond to the demands of the present encounter—the culture of encounter of Pope Francis.

Holiness means self-giving, self-offering, and selfless service of others modeled after the example of Jesus. Christian holiness is always linked with the cross, pouring out our lives in love and service of others.

The distinctive form of priestly holiness is to be found precisely in the priestly ministry and not separate from it. Ministry gives shape to the priest's path of holiness because by ordination, ministry is an essential part of his identity. Ministry and pastoral activities are not a distraction from a priest's spiritual life. Rather, ministry is at the heart of priestly spirituality. A priest finds holiness in the challenges of self-giving precisely as a shepherd after the heart of Christ.

Priestly holiness is formed in a mutually enriching interaction of prayer and ministry. A priest can never hide from pastoral activity by claiming that his prayer must always take priority. Nor, as is more likely in our day, can a priest claim that he doesn't have time for prayer because of the demands of his ministry. Without prayer, there is no ministry, only activity. With prayer, every activity can become an act of love and service, indeed, of prayer. The real formula for success in ministry is the one that St. Ignatius gives us when he tells us, "Pray as if everything depended upon God, work as if everything depended upon you." Unfortunately, too often we only embrace the second part of this great maxim.

The pastoral charity of the priest lived out in his daily ministry is essentially his genuine self-giving in ministry. The priest's charity is an asceticism of selfless availability. The priest's gift of self does not mean that a priest should be negligent in caring for himself. Ministry isn't nearly as effective if the priest is unhealthy, tired, worn out, or burnt out. In fact, his self-giving in ministry requires that he take care of himself so that his pastoral love can be real and vibrant and even joyful. The very concept of Sabbath rest shows that balance in human life is part of God's plan; hence, I am always asking my priests to develop a rule of life that will ensure that balance.

During the Sabbath year, this Jubilee of Mercy, I hope we will wash a lot more feet; but I hope that we will take seriously Jesus's invitation to his first priests on their ordination day: "Could you not pray one hour with me?" I urge you, my priests, to renew your commitment to pray so that you might be truly ministers of the Lord of the Sabbath and allow his holiness to shine forth in the Church.

Holiness is what allows people to glimpse God in our midst; holiness makes our message credible; holiness is what makes ministry truly successful. Prayer allows Sabbath holiness to color each day when we make time and space for God.

Prayer and mercy are the characteristics of Sabbath, of the Jubilee year, and the formula for a blessed priesthood.

22

ONE VOCATION, ONE FORMATION, ONE MISSION

Once I was visited by a priest who was very discouraged. He said, "Bishop, I am the worst priest in the world." I told him that that is quite a distinction. I asked him about his ordination and first Mass. I said, "Did you fight over who was going to be first in line at your ordination? Did you betray Christ for a handful of money? Did you chop off someone's ears with a machete? Did you then run away and hide?" I was, of course, comparing the "worst priest in the world" with the first priests of the world, the apostles.

The vocation of the apostles begins with the joyful discovery of Christ, and with the reckless abandoning of their boats, their nets, and their families, to follow the Lord. It wasn't too long, however, before they were soon in competition with each other and worried about their retirement benefits, like who was going to have the thrones on the right and the left.

For me, one of the most poignant scenes in the Gospels is the apparition of the risen Christ at Easter to the eleven remaining apostles. They're hiding out in the Cenacle with the doors bolted. Suddenly, Christ is among them showing them his wounded hands as if to say, "See how much I love you." The reaction of the apostles certainly must have been one of very conflicted emotions. First, they were overjoyed to see that Jesus was alive and in their midst. Second, they would have felt a profound shame and embarrassment because of their cowardly behavior. The apostles did not surface even to bury Jesus's body after the crucifixion. Had it not been for Nicodemus and Joseph of Arimathea, Jesus's body would have been cast into a common ditch to be savaged by vultures and dogs. But Jesus's love and forgiveness is so great, he does not even remind them of how badly they have behaved, but instead gives them the gift of the Spirit so that these sinners could become wounded healers.

I find immense consolation in the fact that the Gospels give us, not pious platitudes, but a gritty, realistic portrayal of our first priests, the apostles. They were ordinary men, like us, full of humanity and shortcomings and idiosyncrasies. They were entrusted, however, to carry on the most important mission in the history of the world and, despite all their weaknesses, they did an extraordinary job.

I'm sure that all priests at one point have felt a certain envy of the apostles. We imagine how wonderful it would be to be there and hear Jesus's voice, to see his miracles, and to experience the closeness, the companionship, and the joy of being in his presence. It is ironic, however, that the apostles' worst behavior came about while Jesus was still with them. It was only after the Pentecost experience that they go out boldly to proclaim the gospel and to share with the world what they have received.

Like the apostles, priests today are ordinary men called by God and formed for service to his people. The third paragraph of the decree *Presbyterorum Ordinis* translates this reality with the expression, "Taken from among men for the things of God."

As a diocesan bishop, I meet regularly with priests who have been ordained for five or fewer years. We pray, spending an hour in eucharistic adoration, share a meal, and talk about their joys and challenges in their ministry. Because they are seeing the priesthood through fresh eyes, these young priests articulate powerfully so many of the high and low moments that all priests experience.

In 2015, I had the opportunity to ask a group of twenty-seven recently ordained priests to write down their top joys and challenges of priestly ministry. Since these priests entered priestly formation within the last ten years, their responses are a good measure of whether the goals of *Optatium Totus*, *Presbyterorum Ordinis*, and later *Pastores Dabo Vobis* have been realized in the formation and life of priests today.

While this group is just one cohort of priests from one archdiocese in the United States, they captured the joys and challenges that I've been hearing from priests throughout my service as a priest and bishop.

JOYS

The top two joys expressed by these young priests were ministering the sacraments of healing: reconciliation and the anointing of the sick.

One priest wrote that *hearing confessions* "was something that I was worried about doing before my ordination, but it has turned out to be an incredible joy to be able to bring God's healing and forgiveness to people of every type of situation, from children receiving their first penance, to people returning to the sacrament after decades away from it." Another shared that he "had several people who came to confession with destroyed lives (due to sins like abortion or drugs) and [he] saw firsthand how, by the time they left the confessional, their voices changed. God had forgiven them!" A third priest submitted that for him "the ministry of mercy in the confessional is a great joy. I wish that there were ten times the demand for it!"

Pastoral care of the sick and dying is also one of their top joys. From visiting the ill and infirm, to administering the sacrament of anointing of the sick, to praying with a family at a wake, to celebrating a funeral Mass and committal, these young priests cherish bringing the love of Christ and the Church community to those at the end of life. One priest noted that it is a joy to "give hope for those on their deathbed and for their loved ones. Once I entered the hospital room of a woman who was very much afraid of death. She was told that she was going to die and there was nothing else to be done. Yet, after she received the anointing of the sick and the forgiveness of her sins and the viaticum, her face lightened up and she was happy, willing to die, and 'go home!'"

Another young priest commented, "In seminary, I did not consider profoundly the sacrament of the sick, but now I know it to be a singular and intimate moment of encounter, grace, mercy, and peace. I have been fortunate to experience many sick calls and I love going. On one occasion, I passed by a room filled with people. (It was later in the day than my usual visit due to laziness on my part). As I walked in, one of the patient's eight children said, 'Father, you are not going to believe this: Our father is dying, and he went to Mass every day. My sister just said how she wished a priest could be here, then we looked up and saw you.' I gave him viaticum, we prayed, and then sang. Forty minutes later, he died. I was amazed at God's faithfulness and how he used me (even through my laziness) to be with his son. God showed this man and his family that the promise made eighty-eight years before at baptism to be with him always is still true!"

It is no surprise that *celebrating the Eucharist* and *preaching about the Scriptures* have been highlights of these priests' first years of ministry. In recent studies of priestly satisfaction in the United States, 95 percent of priests say that celebrating Mass is a great joy and 80 percent treasure preaching about the word.[1] The Eucharist is the high point of a priest's daily life, and our recently ordained priests experience it as a daily renewal and strengthening of their priestly identity.

Once after Mass many years ago, I was greeting parishioners as they left the Church. One father who was carrying a small child asked the little boy as he pointed to me, "Do you know who that is?" Sometimes children say, God, the pope, Santa Claus, but without missing a beat, the kid says, "He's the communion guy." I like that. *Ex ore infantium*. A priest is the communion guy. In *Pastores Dabo Vobis*, Pope St. John Paul II speaks of the priest as a "man of communion," "the communion guy." It is a marvelous insight into the identity of the priest. Being men of communion begins with our attachment to Christ, the High Priest, the Good Shepherd, the Bridegroom. The Spirit that anointed him and that descended on the apostles at Pentecost has also anointed priests at their ordination. We must know that the Spirit is guiding the Church and is acting in our ministry. It is a joy to be "men of communion" and not private practitioners or "lone rangers," as we say in the United States.

These twenty-seven priests of the Archdiocese of Boston also indicate that their work of *preparing couples for the*

1. Dean R. Hoge, "Satisfaction and Morale among Parish Clergy: What American and Catholic and Orthodox Priests Can Learn from Each Other," paper presented at the Society for the Scientific Study of Religion, Portland, OR, October 20, 2006.

sacrament of marriage and *preparing families for the sacrament of baptism* of their newborn babies are sources of joy. Priests either witness the great faith of couples and families in these moments or can use the opportunity to reintroduce God's love into the daily fabric of family life. One priest mentioned recently working with a couple that wanted to postpone their wedding due to financial reasons. Throughout the course of their conversations, the priest was able to encourage them to reprioritize things and they ended up simplifying their wedding day and focusing on the sacrament and not the reception as the central element. "The ceremony was prayerful, joyful, and worthy of the Lord, especially because it was simplified." Another young priest highlighted how he helped six cohabitating couples to be married last year and to embrace their marriage as a sacrament. This priest was thankful to God to see the fruit of his work of evangelization.

Our young priests also experience joy in their daily opportunities to *witness the power and grace of Jesus working in the lives of people*, comparing it to "having a front-row seat at a sports game." One observed, "It is as if God tells me, 'See how much I love this person.' I sometimes leave my rectory with a heavy heart of tiredness, fears or complaints, but almost without exception, I come back full of joy. I truly see my priestly calling as a way of my sanctification." Another commented that it is a joy each day to be an "instrument of grace, hope, and comfort to many people" who seek out the love of God and his Church. A third added that the "top joy in my life is accompanying a parish community. It is being with the people in their high points and low points and helping them discover, or rediscover, their relationship with God."

These young priests also experience joy from *teaching and sharing the faith with young people*. One wrote that it is often challenging to hold the attention of students preparing for confirmation but then after praying with them, "I marvel at how the Holy Spirit speaks through me to help those kids and how students will seek me out to convey appreciation for what they have learned." Another stated that he recently worked with the youngest students. "A couple of weeks ago before Mass, I gathered all the children at the front of the church to teach them how to genuflect and about the Lord's real presence. Now, it gives me great joy to see them genuflect before the tabernacle before going into their pews." A third priest said that "getting to know my parishioners and students is a tremendous gift to me, as their presence and faith inspires and energizes me."

CHALLENGES

These twenty-seven recently ordained priests, like more than 90 percent of priests, according to recent studies, are substantially happy and joyful. Nevertheless, they were also able to identify challenges that they deal with frequently in their ministry.

Generally, priests face many difficulties today like ministering in a time when the number of priests has declined, and the average age of priests has risen. Often people have high, even unrealistic expectations of priests, for example, there is the consumer mentality by which priests are to provide efficient and friendly service like people expect from salespersons or hotel clerks. Additionally, priests must minister in a culture that is often unfriendly to a faith-centered perspective. Priests must be self-giving in an age of narcissism—a "me-first" attitude—and a culture of entitlement that makes people believe they deserve to be given what earlier generations assumed they had to work for. Priests must preach the gospel in an age in which religious faith, Church authority, and institutional religion are questioned, doubted, and even ridiculed. Priests must strive to lead a chaste life in an age of sexual permissiveness and self-indulgence in a world where sexually explicit material is as accessible as the television or the computer in the next room.

Given all these difficulties, the twenty-seven recently ordained priests indicate that their biggest challenge is one of *time management*—finding time to meet all their requests and to handle the less urgent tasks of outreach to the unchurched, to exercise, to continue their formational learning, and to nourish key relationships. Some of the priests indicate that their daily workload and hard scheduling choices can leave them feeling *overwhelmed and tired*.

One expressed, "My biggest challenge is getting too anxious because of the many things to do. Not the busyness, itself, but the stress, fatigue, and anxiety it can produce." Another remarked, "There are so many needs in parish life and so many people need help that it is very difficult to take care of my own human and spiritual needs. It is hard to relax knowing that there are so many people in dire need. It is not a matter of being the savior of the world; it is more the realization that a simple call or gesture can impact their lives."

A third priest echoed these sentiments, stating, "The greatest challenge is the overabundance of obligations and the lack of time in which to meet them. Serving in multiple parishes, it becomes far too easy to become a sacramental functionary and more difficult to establish deep and meaningful relationships with parishioners. The pastoral presence that I seek isn't easily achieved and legitimate needs, such as evangelistic outreaches like youth groups or men's groups are sacrificed in order to meet other pressing needs."

Another difficulty that parish priests experience is that they can occasionally feel that their job title should be *head of the complaint department*. If we fielded a survey in every parish, we would hear that if a priest is older, parishioners say that he is crotchety; if he is younger, he lacks gravitas. If he preaches for three minutes, they say that he is lazy; if he preaches for ten minutes, he is long-winded. If he redecorates the church, they say that he is extravagant; if he doesn't renovate the place, he is cheap and negligent. If he visits the parishioners, they say that he is nosey; if he doesn't visit parishes, he is aloof. If he dresses casually, they say that he is worldly; if he wears his cassock, he is old-fashioned. If he tells jokes, he is frivolous; if he does not tell jokes, he is too serious. God forbid that he be too fat, or bald, or have a bad singing voice. Everyone wants a good preacher, a great administrator who is also charming. But at the end of the day, people will always admit, "We just want a holy priest."

Some of our young priests experience the difficulty of *low zeal or motivation to grow in faith* on the part of some parishioners. Other priests are confronted with dealing with parishioners who resist pastoral change efforts. Still others face the task of preaching to adults who have been formed by *the prevailing culture to view Church teaching with suspicion*. Many also deal with the reality of *unhealthy gossip* in their parishes.

Another challenge for many of these young priests is *not enough priestly fraternity* in their life. Some describe this in terms of *loneliness*; they are often the only priest in the rectory, and they end up eating alone. Others characterize it as generational differences in the worldview and the pastoral priorities among priests, including in their rectory, leaving them to feel *isolated* and not connected to a supportive community like they have been accustomed to during their formational experiences in seminary.

STRATEGIES FOR GREATER PRIESTLY JOY

Among the presbyterate in Boston, we speak often about these challenges and strategies to overcome them—or at least cope with them. We recognize that business as usual is not enough if we are going to be able to fulfill our mission. We have to go the extra mile, turn the other cheek, give our tunic along with the cloak. Our priestly vocation comes with the grace of the cross, but at the same time, it is a bargain. A priest's life is a beautiful life.

To address many of the above challenges and to promote priestly holiness, I ask each priest of the Archdiocese of Boston to do three things:

1. commit to a serious annual retreat,
2. become part of a priestly support group, and
3. develop a personal *rule of life*.

All three activities—especially the rule of life—can help priests with their time management and to prioritize their challenges. A rule of life is a game plan for a balanced existence and can guarantee that we have time and space for God in our lives. A priest's rule of life will be centered on the celebration of the Eucharist—the high point in the daily life of a priest. A good priestly rule of life includes the intentions of frequent confession, continuing formation, care for one's health with proper diet, exercise, sleep, and an annual medical checkup. A strong rule of life also includes commitment to an hour of prayer each day that should take three forms: the Liturgy of the Hours; favorite devotions like the rosary, stations, or Divine Mercy chaplet; and very importantly, a period of reflective prayer.

Support groups offer priests many benefits. In these gatherings, priests discuss Christ's love for each of us and the sacred mission that he has entrusted to his priests. Some of these groups are called "Emmaus Groups" because the risen Lord draws near and breaks open the Scriptures so much that the experience makes their hearts burn within them. Like the disciples on the road to Emmaus who run back to Jerusalem to share their joy and good news with their brothers, priests often leave Emmaus Groups with a renewed passion for witnessing to their faith in a personal way. In our last meeting of young priests, one man shared with us how he meets regularly with his priests' support group, and they always include three topics among their points of discussion: their prayer life, fidelity to celibacy, and their use of money. He is one of my diocesan priests that studied in our Redemptoris Mater Seminary.

To increase our level of *priestly fraternity and fellowship,* we hold annual convocations and monthly vicariate meetings, in which we discuss how we can become a more intentional presbyterate. Father Ron Knott has encouraged us to return to the ancient theology of an intimate sacramental brotherhood and replace the common and strong notion of priesthood as an individual ministry. At the ordination ceremony, all the priests come forward to lay on hands, and again all come forward to give the kiss of peace. The new priests' hands are anointed with the very chrism that this same presbyterate blessed, together with the bishop, a few months before. All of this indicates our unity as a presbyterate, our oneness with Christ and with each other.

These gatherings of priests can be good opportunities to discuss and renew our priestly identity. When I am present, I often encourage priests *to embrace the missionary aspect of our priestly identity*: we are sent to proclaim the good news to the poor, and especially those who are impoverished by being far from the gospel and the community of faith. We are called to search for the lost. Pope Francis has so effectively reminded us of this mission to reach out to all those on the periphery, to heal their wounds, to walk with them as they take steps to reestablish relationships with God and the Church. Priests can be models of this activity and encourage their parishioners to do the same.

In dealing with challenges of *parish culture, we recommend that our priests confront it directly*. Because some parishioners view their relationship with the Church as consumers, some of our parish communities are maintenance oriented. People come to Church to get something, and they expect the leadership to provide it. All the energy and resources of the parish are oriented to serving the people who are present, rather than reaching out to those who are absent. Our priests know that, over time, we must form our parishioners to help turn them from consumers into disciples and disciple makers who share actively in the mission and ministry of Jesus.

When none of the above coping strategies work, I encourage our priests to *be like Simon of Cyrene and clutch the cross* in our ministry despite ourselves. I have always identified with Simon of Cyrene. He did the noble thing, but reluctantly, under pressure. He was pressed into service. He was embarrassed to be part of an execution, angry because he was innocent and forced to be part of a spectacle. He was afraid of what damage would be done to his standing in the community, in his family. I like to think that later Simon of Cyrene looked back on that horrific experience of carrying Christ's cross up Mount Calvary through a hostile crowd as the defining moment in his life. He looked back with gratitude for the privilege of carrying Christ's cross. His sons, Rufus and Alexander, surface in Acts and Mark and the Epistles. He must have embraced the faith and passed it to his family. Like Simon, as priests we must overcome our fears of suffering, of failure, of shame, of sickness, of death, and of being alone. We can do so in prayer and reflection on Christ's love for each of us and on the gift of ministry, especially when it is most difficult. We can grow from being reluctant Cyrenians to being more like Veronica, who overcame fear, human respect, and personal safety to bring a moment of relief to the suffering Christ.

CONCLUSION

Christ has made us priests because he loves us, not because we are good looking, clever, or holy, but because he loves us. A priestly vocation is a vocation to love.

One of our young priests wrote, "I feel great fulfillment in exercising ministerial priesthood in Christ's name. Even though we live in tough times, Jesus did too, and I find joy in walking in his footsteps."

I began by reflecting on the human qualities of the first priests, the apostles. Though priests today have not had the privilege of walking over the hills of Galilee in Jesus's company, we have received the same Spirit that the apostles did on Holy Thursday, on Easter Sunday, and at Pentecost. And now our priestly mission continues, despite the weaknesses and shortcomings of his priests and the challenges we face in our ministry. Christ is counting on today's priests as he counted on those simple fishermen to preach his gospel, calling people to conversion and discipleship, and building a community of faith around the Eucharist. Like those first Christians in the Acts of the Apostles, priests must be united in embracing the teachings of the apostles, fellowship and prayer, and the breaking of the bread. Let us walk forward with the certain hope that God will always provide laborers for the harvest and will walk with us through the joys and challenges of priestly life.

Convention of the Congregation for Clergy,
Pontifical Urban University, 2015